MW01224127

This is a work of creative nonfiction. Some parts have been fictionalized in varying degrees, for various purposes.

Copyright © 2020 by Grant Waldie
Denver, CO
USA

FIRST EDITION

Cover Design by Grant Waldie

www.SelfTaughtMBA.com

ISBN 979-8-63-719868-9 (paperback)
ASIN B08761NCB7 (paperback)
ASIN B0873Z51QS (ebook)

Published by Amazon Kindle Direct Publishing
kdp.amazon.com

Thank you to my wife, Karlye.

Without you encouraging me to write a book, I never would have even tried.

I love you

Random Advice
for
Business & Life

Grant Waldie, B.A.Sc.

Contents

Section Five: How to Manage a Project

Section Six: How to Improve your Work Life

Section Seven: Leadership

Section Eight: Running a Company

Sorry... 261

Epilogue 265

Introduction:

People have been giving me advice my whole life.

"Look before you cross the street", "Wash your hands", "Don't talk to strangers" – it starts from back when I was as young as I can remember.

A few years ago, I was reflecting on my life and career and I wondered why it was that I got to the place where I was at and other people that I grew up with got to a different place.

Some people soared to heights far above what I'll ever achieve, and some are stuck in the same place they were at after they graduated.

What separates those that "Make it" and those that don't? Have I "Made it"? What's the definition of "Making it"? This is a deeper philosophical argument and one that I don't plan on even attempting to answer with this book.

I started to keep track of all the advice I would get. I also thought back to teachers that I had, family members, friends, bosses, religious teachers, people on TV, books I've read, and all the various life experiences that have taught me lessons and given me advice and I started to make a list.

After a few months of adding to this list I circulated it around the office to my coworkers. They started to add to the list. The list started to grow and grow.

Then, in the year 2020, a disease called "COVID-19" started to infect people all over the world. The United States (and many other countries) went on lock-down. Millions of people were told to stay home.

My wife encouraged me to write a book with all my free time stuck at home. I immediately thought of this list that my colleagues and I had been cultivating over the past few years.

What you have before you is the culmination of a number of years of creating a list of small pieces of advice from across everyone I've ever met…and thanks to a quarantine, I finally had time to put it into book form. Some of it is my advice, some is others…I hope you enjoy it.

Section One:
Improving Yourself

Personal Motto Part 1

I was once talking to a good friend of mine and she said her personal motto was "Do what you're good at to make the world a better place."

I love that motto. The tricky part of it though is that you can parse that sentence into three parts that are all up for discussion.

"Do what you're good at..."

How many of us have watched the popular TV show "American Idol"? I think the most watched episodes of that show are the first few when they are auditioning thousands of people from all across the country. How many of those people standing in line think they are good at singing? I think they all do. How many are? Not many.

Just because you think you are good at something does not mean that you actually are. It's tough to figure out if you are in fact good at something. You ask your significant other "Do you think I'm a good singer?" and they emphatically say "YES!"...because they don't want an argument or to hurt your feelings. This can be said about most talents that people have or do not have.

One good way of finding out if you are actually good at something is to ask someone that hates you if you are in fact good at the thing. If they say "Well, yeah, you're actually a really good singer, but I still hate you and you still owe me money" then you know they're telling the truth...and also make sure you pay them back the money you owe them.

It is tough to figure out what you are actually good at, but once you've figured that out, we move onto the next part of the phrase:

"...to make the world..."

What is your world? Some of us can affect the entire world. I recently saw a billboard that said "Anyone who thinks they can't change the whole world never ate an undercooked bat." I hope this book lives on long enough that you don't understand the joke. We are currently under lock-down quarantined to our apartments as the world suffers through a pandemic virus that was allegedly caused by someone being exposed to a bat. Don't eat bats.

But for most of us, the "world" is our neighbors, our coworkers, our family and friends. Our "world" is maybe a hundred or a thousand people. It's tough to say, but everyone we can affect is in our world.

"...a better place."

This is the toughest part of the phrase. What is a better place? If you are a religious missionary who follows religion X, you would think that converting people to X will make the world a better place. But if you follow religion Y, then "a better place" is when everyone is a Y-follower. Regardless of X and Y being religion, or political party, or diet, or exercise, or way of life, your way is not necessarily the way the whole world should do it, and if the whole world did it your way, that might not necessarily be "better."

These three things are tricky to find the answers to. What are you good at? Who do you have the power to affect? Will your effect make things better?

I can't solve those questions for you, but they are a good starting point for you to ponder. If more people in the world were honestly trying to make the world better for others that would be a net-positive, even if there are a few bad-singing misguided people out there who are trying to convert us to X.

SUMMARY: Do what you're good at to make the world a better place.

Bookworm Part 1

There's an endless stream of Netflix, Hulu, Crave, Disney+, YouTube, Instagram, Twitter, TikTok, FaceBook and other distractions out there. Your phone never seems to stop blowing up. Your alerts and notifications don't stop.

It's time to slow down…and read a book.

Do I say this because I write books and I'm hoping you keep me employed? No, not at all. Well, maybe kinda sorta.

But seriously – you need to read more.

And don't give me that "I don't have the time." Yes you do. You get 24 hours every single day. 8 of them should be spent sleeping, 8 of them will most likely be spent working. That means there are literally 8 other hours every single day.

Where do those hours go?

It's amazing that we get 8 hours to ourselves every day and yet we still somehow fill them.

Yes, kids take up a lot of time. If you are in a relationship and you want to maintain it that will also take many hours out of your day.

These things are worth your time, but so is reading.

Don't start with Wealth of Nations (or don't ever read it – I have, it's pretty boring).

Start with books that are 150-300 pages max.

Start with non-fiction books. Non-fiction books can be picked up and put down and you can keep getting something from them each time you read them. Alternately, works of fiction need to be read in chronological order and you need to keep at it otherwise you'll forget the storyline.

I would suggest you spend time in the business, self-help, philosophy, psychology, or opinion section of your local bookstore. Or scan the best sellers list on Amazon of these same topics.

What is great about those types of books is that you can almost always read those types of books in any order you want, skip sections you find boring, come back to things you like, and they are also generally quite short reads.

Commit to reading for 30 minutes each night. That's the same length of time a sitcom is.

If you can bump it up to 1 hour a night, that's great! But don't overdo it. 1 hour of reading a day is a very very healthy amount of reading for you to do.

Look at a list of successful people in the world: Bill Gates, Elon Musk, Warren Buffet, Barack Obama, Tom Hanks, Oprah – they all talk about how much they love reading and how much it has helped them in life.

If you want a list to get your started, I put together a website of my favorite business and self-help books.

Check out www.SelfTaughtMBA.com

SUMMARY: Spend more time reading books.

Arnold

Arnold Schwarzenegger did not invent bodybuilding, but he certainly was one of the major contributors who made it popular.

In 1977, Arnold was the star of an indie film called *"Pumping Iron."* If you haven't seen it, and even if you are not a fan of bodybuilding or Arnie, I highly recommend you check it out.

This movie launched the fitness revolution.

Nowadays, you can't go anywhere without being inundated with advertisements for gyms, exercise studios, yoga classes, rec league sports teams, workout devices, and every other fitness craze under the sun.

And yet, YOU still don't get enough exercise.

(Or maybe you do. If you do, you can skip this chapter)

But seriously – are you exercising enough?

Are you eating properly?

You know the answer to this. You know where you are falling short.

Life keeps going and going and when you start eating healthy, stop drinking alcohol, stop drinking coffee, stop doing drugs, stop smoking, and start exercising, your life gets better.

You know this. Stop kidding yourself.

Quitting bad habits is hard. I get that. But you can always try to quit that bad habit again. You don't have to run a marathon but doing literally ANYTHING other than the nothing that you are currently doing will be good for you.

It's never ever too late to start. You can start exercising or quit that bad habit or start eating right TODAY. You just need a little encouragement and hopefully this chapter will be the gentle kick in the pants that you needed.

SUMMARY: Stop drinking alcohol and coffee, stop smoking, stop taking drugs, start exercising and start eating healthy.

Heart Attack

At work, there are occasional blow-ups.

We've all been doing something a certain way for a while and we all know that this is going to go wrong eventually, but until that does happen we just keep going along with it.

Then suddenly, BOOM, the thing that we all knew was going to happen finally happens.

Maybe we've all been putting the wrong number on our timesheet and now accounting needs all of us to work overtime to go back through all our timesheets to correct it. This is going to take 5 hours per person and we all have to do it on a Thursday night before payroll on Friday.

Or maybe we've been using that same tool at work with the loose safety guard. It's going to fall off eventually. We all know it. We are putting our life in danger each time we use it.

Finally, one day, the guard falls off and it badly injures a coworker.

We saw it coming. We all knew it was going to happen. And yet, we did nothing to stop it.

Stop doing that.

How many people eat unhealthy food and smoke and drink and have their doctor tell them that they need to stop, otherwise they are going to have a heart attack? Their cholesterol is off the charts, they have trouble breathing when they have to walk up stairs, and yet they keep living their unhealthy lifestyle.

Then what happens? They have a heart attack.

For many people, this is the wakeup call that they need. For the real idiots in the world, even a near-death experience won't convince them that they need to change things up.

But what about the people that saw it coming and still chose to do nothing?

They are just as stupid as the others.

Yes, you could take this chapter to be talking about literal physical health. If so, that's great. But I'm moreso pointing it at all the messed up things we are doing in our corporate environment that we know are not the right things to do but we just keep on doing them.

What are you putting off at work that you know is going to come back to bight you in the ass? What things are being done the wrong way and someone someday is going to make you work a massive amount of overtime to correct them?

Start working on correcting those things right now.

SUMMARY: Don't wait for a heart attack to start living healthy (literal or figurative or both).

Maintenance

Many of us spend thousands of dollars on our vehicle. Tricking it out with enhanced speakers and entertainment systems, fancy wheels, paint jobs, souped-up engines, and other modifications.

Or maybe we are obsessed about remodeling our house or interior decorating. The bedsheets need to be perfect, the theatre room has to have the largest TV on the block, the kitchen needs all the newest gadgets and cabinets, and that bathroom must be fit for royalty.

We spend a lot of time and a lot of money on various physical possessions, yet we tend to neglect our own body.

I'm not talking about working out and eating right, I'm talking about those minor medical procedures that you know you should probably get done, but you've just been putting them off.

Maybe there's a couple of small moles / skin tags you should get removed. Have you considered laser eye surgery? Do those wisdom teeth hurt but you keep them in? Are your teeth just a bit crooked but you're too scared to try invisible braces? Does that knee keep bothering you but you don't want to get the surgery?

There are many small elective surgeries that would not only improve our day-to-day life, but also possibly extend our life.

We are quick to drop thousands of dollars to remodel our home or trick out our car, yet we don't want to spend far less to have a minor surgery.

As we get older, these small elective surgeries become less elective and more a necessity. Even just learning how your body responds to anesthetics, medicines, and what your healing time is could become very important for when you need to get emergency surgery later in life. Stop putting it off, call up a doctor today and book a consultation for that small surgery you've been putting off.

SUMMARY: Get that minor surgery or procedure that you've been putting off.

Levels

There are so many things to think about. Just look at this book. There is a ton of advice located in these pages, and I even occasionally point to other books I think you should read that they themselves will have even more lists of advice.

Where do you start? How do you not get overwhelmed?

I have found that it is and always will be a constant struggle. Life is complicated and has a lot of twists and turns. I don't always win, but I do spend a lot of my time reflecting on what areas I need to adjust the levels in.

I can't make your list for you – you need to do that. Many of the pieces of advice in this book you will find obvious and you are already doing. Hopefully though, there are a few areas you are probably lacking in and this book will hopefully give you that little extra boost that you need to finally make that change.

I like to keep track of areas in my life that are important to me, and ask myself if I'm putting enough effort into them, or am I putting too much effort in and spending too much time. Currently, my personal list looks something like this:

Exercise, Diet, Chiropractor/Massage, Reading, Writing, Calling Friends/Family, Spending quality time with my wife, Work, Studying for that next course, Travel, Charity, Playing music, sleeping in / napping / relaxing.

That's my current personal list. I can tell you that I'm doing really well in seven of those categories, pretty good in three of them, and falling short in three of them. I've got to adjust my levels. I'm spending a bit too much time in some areas, and not nearly enough effort in other areas.

Your life is complicated, just like mine. Make a list, and figure out where you need to adjust the levels.

SUMMARY: Continuously adjust the levels of where you are focusing your time, energy, and efforts.

Jesus

Jesus said a lot of things. Whether you are a devout Christian who centers their life around the teachings of Christ, or an atheist that thinks the stories of Jesus are greatly exaggerated and/or completely made up, you have to admit that there definitely are some good words of wisdom and advice in the writings that are said to be about his teachings.

One line that Jesus said goes something a bit like this: *"Why do you look at the speck of sawdust in your brother's eye and pay no attention to the plank in your own eye? ...You hypocrite, first take the plank out of your own eye, and then you will see clearly to remove the speck from your brother's eye."*

I had a high school teacher who had his own way of saying the same thing: *"Figure out your own shit first."*

Some people think it's selfish to focus on your own things. They want to be seen as always helping other people. It's certainly nice to help others, but if you yourself are a mess, what are you doing trying to help others? You need to get your own house in order first.

Giving money to charity, baking or cooking for someone who is in need, helping someone with their gardening, taking care of someone's kids to give them a night off – all these things are great and you can certainly do these at all times.

However, "giving people advice" is often a way that people think they are "helping."

If you are going to give others advice on money, you better be rich. If you are going to tell others how to be healthy, you better be healthy. This is where the "Take the plank out of your own eye" advice comes in.

We have a lot of people in this world who are a mess, yet they can't stop telling others how to live their life.

SUMMARY: Make sure you have your shit figured out before you start telling people how to live their life.

Optimization

There are things that we do over and over again, day after day. Yet despite doing these same things every day, we don't optimize them, and thus we waste time.

It may be something simple, but when you add it up over your lifetime, it can make a big difference.

Steve Jobs wore the same clothes every day because he hated wasting time picking out an outfit. Mark Zuckerberg does the same thing. Maybe this doesn't work for you because you love fashion. That's ok. Ask yourself though, how is your closet organized? Do you have all the dressy clothes on one side, and the casual clothes on the other? Or is it a mess? If you aren't optimizing the way you organize your closet, you will spend more time trying to find that perfect outfit not because you can't decide on the color, but simply because you literally can't find the shirt you want.

Do you drive an hour to work every day? That is a huge waste of time. You need to either find a job that is closer to where you want to live, or find a place to live that's closer to where you work. Or maybe you need to work from home.

Do you walk aimlessly all over the grocery store going up and down an aisle, only to have to go back to that same aisle? Instead of looking through a list and running all over the store, you should be going up and down aisles systematically so you aren't wasting time.

By freeing up time in areas that don't matter, you give yourself more time to relax, read, watch TV, spend time with family/friends, exercise, or other things that are far more enjoyable than searching for a shirt.

Yes, it can be difficult to get into the habit of optimizing your life, but it pays massive dividends if you keep at it.

SUMMARY: Optimize the tasks that you do repeatably in order to save time, lessen frustration, and overall improve your life.

Reflections

We live in a world of go go go. Endless notifications and distractions. How do productive people get so much more accomplished, when they have the exact same number of hours in each day?

One trick I learned a long time ago was to take time to reflect on what I got accomplished, what I am currently working on, and where do I want to go. The problem becomes, how much time do I spend doing this and when do I do it?

Depending on what you are reflecting on will determine the amount of time you spend reflecting. Are you thinking about today? That should take you seconds. Unless today was a big day and you had a big moment, you should be able to summarize the day's ups and downs in 5 seconds.

What about your week? You had that thing you wanted to get done. Did you do it? Why not? A weekly reflection might take a minute.

How about this month. You originally committed to yourself that you were going to do X at least once a week this whole month. If you fell behind, what can you do differently to make next month better? This internal discussion may take a number of minutes and you might have to come back to it.

Bill Gates has had, since he started Microsoft, an entire week dedicating to thinking/reflecting. He does this once a year. One of the richest, most successful humans to ever live thought that an entire week of self-reflection made sense to do once a year. Maybe you do the same? Maybe you take a two or three week trip? Maybe you just dedicate a solid weekend. Whatever you do, if you want to follow in the footsteps of Bill Gates and other success stories, you need to take time to stop and reflect on where you are and where you want to be.

SUMMARY: Every day/week/month/year, spend an appropriate amount of time reflecting on your day/week/month/year. Think about where you are, and where you want to be.

No Service

I once went on a three-week trip throughout Asia with no SIM card so my cellphone wouldn't work and I only used my phone for photos. It was some of the best three weeks of my life.

I went with one of my best friends. He got to Asia one week ahead of me and started the trip in Taiwan. He had a childhood friend who lived there and had free accommodation via his buddy. His buddy had a sister whose job it was to go to nightclubs and party with all her other friends. I'm not sure if the general public is aware of this, but yes, that's a real job. Night clubs pay girls to come each night, dance, laugh, and have a good time. It's good for business.

He spent the entire week partying every night. They got into all the clubs with no cover charge and never waited in line. The five or so girls were super fun to be around and laughed at all of his stories.

From that week-long party he joined me in Beijing, China. I had just gotten off an 18-hour flight and was exhausted. When trying to find a taxi at the airport, a polite gentleman approached me and said (in perfect English) "Hello sir, are you looking for a taxi?"

I was looking for a taxi, so I followed him and got in his car.

I failed to notice that there was no "TAXI" sign on the top of the car and there was no meter. I had just gotten into some random dude's car...and for some reason there was his buddy sitting beside him in the front seat.

I showed him the address and he told me the taxi ride would cost $50 US dollars. I was half asleep so I didn't care.

We drove for 30 minutes and we showed up to the hotel. I had booked this hotel on points. It was totally free. However, the "taxi" driver didn't know that. What he saw was that we had just pulled up to the Beijing Grand Hilton – the most expensive hotel in China. His buddy said to me "It's $100 US dollars if you want your bags back."

Now, granted, one hundred bucks is not an insane amount of money to pay to get all my belongings back. And I was very tired. And I had no other choice. Did I just start off the trip by getting kinda mugged? And did my friend start off his trip with pretty girls laughing at his jokes for a week straight? I think one of us made the wrong decision.

I met up with my friend in the hotel room and we went to bed. We attempted to watch TV but every single channel was the President of China making a speech. By reading the subtitles I learned that "China" is not pronounced "China" in China. In fact, there's no relationship between what Westerners call that country and what people from that country call that country.

The name "China" is actually derived from the Qin Dynasty. But when someone from China says "Qin" it sounds like they are saying "Chin." During the silk road trade period in history, people would say "This is from Chin-a" which, over time, became "China."

There are literally millions of people in China that have no idea what the rest of the world is saying when they say "China." They call their country "Zhongguo" which is pronounced "Jung go-a" which means "Central Nation."

We went to sleep and woke up early the next morning to head to the Great Wall of China.

Because we woke up at 4:00 am we were able to get to the wall at sunrise. There was no one there. We were the very first people that day. For the next 45 minutes, we ran around the walled city and went up and down the outreaches that made up that section of the wall. We got amazing photos with no one in the background. It was an incredible experience.

Then the tourists started to show up, so we left.

Fun Fact: The Great Wall is not, and never was, one continuous wall. If you saw it mapped out, it looks more like someone took wet noodles and threw them on a plate. The goal of the wall was not to be one continuous barrier, but rather it was to funnel invading troops to areas where battles could be more easily won because the defending side would have the higher ground.

We left the Great Wall and headed to the Beijing Central Train Station. Our goal was to go to Tibet and we were 50/50 sure we would actually make it there.

Going to Tibet is illegal. Or, as Kramer would say it "It's not illegal, it's just against the law."

When we were first signing up for our China VISAs, we had to show on our application form our detailed itinerary. I had read online that we aren't allowed to go to Tibet so I phoned up the Chinese embassy in my home city. The woman on the phone said to me "If you mention Tibet on your application form, you will be denied for life to ever go to China." I thanked her, hung up the phone, and felt lucky that I called from my work phone and not my personal cellphone.

I then googled "How to go to Tibet" and found that the way to do it is to make up a fake itinerary. You show this to the VISA application people, and you get your VISA.

I created a fake itinerary that had me and my buddy going through Beijing, Shanghai, and Hong Kong. With all the fun stops I put in he remarked "This trip sounds almost better than our real trip!"

I went to the VISA application center and the man there said to me "Let's see your hotel reservations, plane tickets and train tickets." Not only do I have to make up a fake itinerary, I actually have to go ahead and book it!

So I did. I booked an entire three-week trip that my buddy and I would never go on. I went back to the VISA application center, showed all the documents to the guy, and we both got our VISAs. Once we had the VISA in our passport, we cancelled all our hotels and train tickets.

This gets us into China, but does not get us into Tibet. For that, we found a guy online that said he specialized in sneaking people into Tibet. If we would PayPal him thousands of dollars, he said he would get us train tickets from Beijing to Tibet and take care of all the hotels and tours while we were there.

Does this sound sketchy to you? It did to us, but sometimes in life you have to take some chances. We sent him the money and he sent us some PDFs to print out that were all in Chinese. We had no idea what they said, but we had trust in humanity that this would all work out.

Fast forward to the Beijing Train Station. We've just come from the Great Wall and now we are standing in line for the train. We hand a piece of paper to a lady working there. She says something to us in Chinese. We don't speak Chinese. She pauses, then she points at the train. We take this as our cue to get on board.

We were in "First Class." This means there are two bunkbeds per room. My friend was on the bottom bunk, I was on the top, and a random couple was on the other two beds.

"Second Class" was the same setup, except instead of bunk beds of two, they were bunk beds of three – 6 beds per room. However, most of the beds had two people lying in them. 12 people per room.

"Third Class" was just seats. Three on the right side, and three on the left side, with an aisle that separates them. Old people, young people, chickens, dogs, and probably some other animals were in third class. It smelt the way you would think it would smell.

If you had a First Class ticket, you were allowed to go into Second and Third Class. Second Class ticket holders could go into Third Class. Third Class could not leave their cabin.

I walked the entire length of the train. I counted the number of people per row, multiplied it by the number of rows, and multiplied it by the number of cars. I did the same thing for Second and First Class. When I was done, I reported back to my friend: This train has 1,500 people on it and you and I are the only two white guys.

There were no toilets in Third Class (I guess they got off at stops and went?) Second Class had a hole in the floor that was disgusting. First Class had the same hole, but it was much cleaner.

The best part of First Class was that we had access to the dining car. We spent most of our three-day trip across China there.

When we first went in, we noticed that everyone got menus handed to them…except us. At first I thought they had run out of menus. Then, another person entered the car and got a menu. I see what's happening here. They think we don't speak Chinese (we don't) so they think it's pointless to hand us an all-Chinese menu.

I got up and grabbed a menu. We had pre-downloaded onto our phone a translation app that would take the Chinese characters and put them into English. The English wasn't great, but it was passable. The first thing on the menu was "Spicy chicken fun time." That sounds pretty good to me. The second item was "Black death mold." That could be a mistranslation of "Mushroom soup" but it was China so there's a good possibility that it in fact was actually black death mold.

We used this method for the rest of the trip. We pointed at items on the menu and the waiter always seemed to figure it out. We had some of the best food we've ever had in my life on that train. It deserved a Michelin Star.

The receipt was always in written Chinese. Instead of $15 it would say "fifteen" but in Chinese. Our translation app did not work on scribbled Chinese. To solve this, I would always give 100 Chinese dollars, which was roughly $15 US dollars, and we always seemed to get change. Everyone was happy. We had a system figured out.

Our train arrived in Tibet. We got off and met up with other Westerners. Our group was 12 large, led by a local Tibetan.

Over the next 3 days we travelled to numerous monasteries and learned the history of Tibet. However, the history stopped in 1966. That is the year the leader of China, Mao Zedong started the "Cultural Revolution." Its stated goal was to purge China of all capitalist and traditional elements from Chinese society. This was immediately after "The Great Leap Forward" which saw 30 million people die. Feel free to google it and read Wikipedia's large description of the time.

Regardless, our tour guide did not talk about it. For one, it's a sad time in which he would have lost family members, and for second, there were

Chinese military guards all around us listening in on our tours – I'm quite certain they wouldn't want tourists knowing about this piece of Chinese history.

We continued to tour monasteries until three members of our group got arrested. Yes, that's right – three random Westerners got arrested.

Their official crime was "Protesting the Government." What was it that they actually did? They took the wrong photo.

The group of three was a family from Portugal. The dad worked an office job, the son was in middle school, and the daughter was 21. They were fans of soccer and they had a banner that said "I love Portuguese Football." They held up this banner as they stood in front of a government building. Within seconds, members of the military started questioning them. They don't speak Chinese, the military don't speak Portuguese, and both of them barely speak English. This was not going to go well.

They got arrested, put into the back of a van, and taken away.

What was the reaction of our tour guide? He shrugged and said to the group "You always lose a few."

Three hours later we all met up back at the hotel and the family had returned. We asked them what had happened. They said that they went down to some military building, two officers yelled at them in Chinese for a couple of hours, and then let them go.

The dad said "We like adventure. As a family, we love getting into crazy situations. This was fun!"

We all went out for dinner and I made sure to sit next to this family because I'm sure they had more stories to tell.

I started with the standard question of "So, what do you do for a living?" As I mentioned above, the dad worked an office job, the son was in school, but when it came to the 21 year-old daughter, she hesitated.

She then said "Well, I do not know the way to say in English. My job is...I am a...escort? Is that how you say it?"

I replied "Well...um...maybe? How about you tell me what you do at your job and I'll tell you if you're using the correct word?"

She then said to me "Ok, well, um, lots of older men, they give me money, they buy me gifts, they take me on trips, and then I have the sex with them. Escort? Is that how you say escort?"

I paused.

"Yes. Yes, that is how you say escort."

Her dad was sitting right beside her eating his soup. He paused from the soup and said "It makes GREAT money!"

This, of course, strikes anyone who grew up in America as being pretty strange. A dad who is totally ok with his daughter being a prostitute? How could this be?

However, take a step back and consider the cultural differences around the world. If your daughter was pursuing her modelling career, how would you describe that to someone from Saudi Arabia? You would say something like "My daughter puts on lingerie, has photos taken of her, and people then buy the lingerie."

Imagine the shock on some people's faces who come from very conservative countries.

True, being paid to have sex is on another level, but it's along the same path. We all have different ideas of morality and what is acceptable. This family drew the line in a different place than many of us would, but they seemed happy about it. Who am I to judge?

We finished our trip in Tibet and left for the airport. Nothing too exciting happened there other than when I was going through customs the border guard yelled at me in Chinese and left with my passport. I stood there for the next ten minutes, not able to go anywhere because they put you in these little glass cages when you are standing at the border guard's desk. He eventually came back and handed me my passport. I have no idea what he was checking.

We flew out of Tibet and landed in Nepal. We spend the next week hanging out at the hostel talking to people who were there to go on a trek or climb a mountain.

Almost everyone assumed that we were also there to climb. I had an interest in climbing, but I had no idea how I would fare with elevation. I was born at sea level and at the time I lived at sea level. How would my body react when I went up to 10,000 or 20,000 feet?

I saw many couples there who were in top physical shape. However, one of them was suffering from altitude sickness. They had paid all this money, bought all this gear, taken a ton of time off work, travelled halfway around the world, and now one of them has splitting headaches because they can't deal with elevation sickness.

At the time, I had thoughts of one day climbing Mount Everest, but I had already thought that I should test out my reaction to elevation before I commit to such a task.

Luckily for me, I didn't feel the elevation at all. No headaches, no pain. My week in Nepal was spent relaxing in the sun, doing some short hikes, and talking with other travelers.

This trip to Nepal's and Tibet's elevation gave me the push I needed to start training to climb mountains. I went on to climb Mount Rainier and Mount Kilimanjaro. I then attempted Aconcagua, which is the tallest mountain in the Western Hemisphere. I unfortunately did not make it to the top of that mountain due to my left eyeball freezing (it healed after it thawed) just two hours shy of the summit, forcing me to turn around.

Rainier, Kilimanjaro, and Aconcagua are full of other stories, which I'll share in hopefully a follow-up edition to this book.

Why did I tell you the story of my trip to Asia?

Because I had no phone and I had one of the best times of my life. My brain was, for the first time ever, able to shut off and not think about work. I literally forgot passwords and had to look them up (good thing I write them down). I was able to completely de-stress because I took a real vacation. A vacation is not a vacation if you bring your laptop or you check your phone. You need to unplug. Being plugged in constantly is literally killing you. My wife and I do "Social Media Free Sundays" where we do not check FaceBook, Instagram, Twitter, or any other site. Especially in the world we are currently living in, every post seems to be about more people dying from COVID-19. This isn't healthy to constantly be filling our brains with negative info. It's time to turn off.

Don't be that person in the meeting that is on your phone all the time. It's time for the meeting. Put your phone in your pocket, in your bag, or put it face down on the table.

You have to decide what's best for you in terms of how long you want to disconnect for. For me, it's two to three weeks once a year, plus one day a week, plus an hour or so a day. Do what works for you, but please don't tell me you are connected 24/7/365. You're going to burn out.

SUMMARY: You need to disconnect occasionally. Turn the phone off. I do a two to three weeks per year no-phone vacation, plus one day a week (Sunday), plus an hour or so a day with no access to a phone. You need to do this to keep your sanity.

GQ

This chapter is probably directed moreso to males than females, but the overall point can still be relevant to women.

How do you dress? What is your fashion sense? Do you pay any attention to style, grooming, or fitness?

I know a lot of guys that don't. They somehow take it as a point of pride that they don't care at all what they look like. This actually isn't true. They do care what they look like – they want to look like a slob.

Do you think it helps you to dress like an idiot? Do people want to give you a promotion and a raise because you smell bad? Is your boss much more likely to get you to lead the next team because you are out of shape and don't take care of yourself?

Of course not.

And yet, so many of us don't seem to care what we wear. We put on the exact same ill-fitting pants each day, wear shoes that are comfortable but look like something an out-of-work teenager would wear, our hair is a mess, we shower rarely because "No one has said anything to me" and we generally don't care about what we look like.

Some of us are perfectly content with our ho-hum lives and don't want to change.

If you're in that boat, it's time to smarten up. What the hell are you doing, man? Get a proper haircut and wash your hair regularly. Wear proper clothes to work. If you actually care about your looks this can only help you at work. Many times it might be purely sub-conscious, or maybe it's even completely conscious, but people want to give raises to, promotions to, or generally just work with people that care about their looks.

SUMMARY: Buy better clothes. Get a proper haircut and keep it clean. Exercise and actually care about the way you look. Stop being a slob.

Audiobooks

This may be the only chapter that doesn't have a fairly vague title.

Some people hate reading. If you are one of these people, I'm somewhat doubting you are even reading these words. I did try to make each chapter very short and to-the-point so perhaps I've kept your attention this whole time. Yay!

I suspect that there are many people out there who struggle with reading. They should try audiobooks.

Many audiobooks are completely free. There are summarized versions of popular books as well so you don't have to sit through eight hours to get the best insights from the latest Malcolm Gladwell book.

Audiobooks can be combined with other activities as well. Commuting to work, cooking, or going for a run – audiobooks help you kill two birds with one stone.

We all have smartphones, so put your phone to work and listen to your next book. Make it a habit and crank through more books than you ever could the traditional reading way.

SUMMARY: Start listening to audiobooks. Maybe do it during your commute, while cooking/cleaning, or while exercising.

Mistakes were Made

When Thomas Edison was attempting to invent the lightbulb it is said that he tried over 1,000 times. When asked if he saw this as 1,000 failures he said "I did not fail 1,000 times – I learned 1,000 things that don't work."

We learn far more from our failures than from our successes.

When everything goes right, we don't know if we actually did the right thing, or if we got lucky. When everything goes wrong, we have learned for certain what does not work.

This book is a collection of random pieces of advice that I have curated over the years. Yes, many of the stories are from my own personal life, but I think at least half of them are from other people's lives. Things go wrong all the time in our lives. Are we stepping back to think about what could have been different and how a small critical decision changed it all? Or are we not evaluating things ever?

If we make mistakes and don't take time to think about them and plan for how we are going to do things differently in the future, then that is the real mistake.

As you read this book, hopefully many of the pieces of advice are going to resonate with you. Hopefully it will be the kick in the pants you will need to finally stop doing that thing you know you shouldn't be doing but you've needed a final piece of motivation to finally kick the habit.

You are going to have multiple other life lessons as you get older. Are you writing them down? If you have a hardcopy of this book, feel free to use some of the blank pages at the end to start your own list. Heck, if you think the advice is applicable to an audience outside of yourself, feel free to send it to me and I'll include it in the next volume of this book.

The important thing to remember is that we need to learn from our mistakes and the mistakes of others. If we don't learn a lesson, that is the real tragedy.

SUMMARY: Learn from other's mistakes and keep a list of things NOT to do.

Diversify

Do you remember back in high school when you were learning literally anything, someone at the back of the class would put up their hand and ask "Why do we have to learn this stuff?"?

I remember that question being asked over and over again. I also remember the *wrong* answer being given over and over again.

In math class, we might have been learning how to factor a polynomial. Do you remember that phrase? Dig deep into your memory bank and I'm sure those words at least sound somewhat familiar. The question of "Why is this important?" is asked and the teacher says "Well, um...let's say you have $2x^2 + 3x - 9$ and you really want to know how that breaks down into the form $(x+y)(x-z)$...um...yeah. Then that's why we need to know this!"

What a stupid answer. No wonder kids hate math.

Or maybe we're in English class and someone questions the validity of learning Shakespeare. No one talks like that anymore, so what's the point?

"Because I'm getting paid to teach it to you" was an answer an exacerbated teacher once told our class.

It pains me that the actual answer to this question isn't taught in teacher training school. I think if it was taught, we'd have a lot more interested students.

Here's why we need to learn "pointless" stuff in school, and why you as an adult need to keep learning pointless things if you want to excel in business and life:

(let's give an example)

Sydney Crosby was one of the best hockey players of all time. He set the record for the youngest team captain to ever win a Stanley Cup at the age of 21. He has numerous other records and many second-place records only to "The Great One" Wayne Gretzky.

There is no doubt that he is a great hockey player.

But you know what he is also great at? Soccer.

You know what he is also great at? Basketball.

You know what he is also great at? Golf.

He does not limit the sports that he plays. He does not limit his physical exercises. When he's in the gym, he's working out all of his muscle groups, not just the ones that help him shoot. Hockey is a full-body sport. He has to work out every inch of his body to be in top physical form.

Just as this concept applies to our bodies, it applies to our minds as well.

Our brains are a muscle. Every time we learn something, neurological pathways are connected within the brain, the same way muscle tissue builds on other muscle tissue. Each new thing we learn opens up new pathways throughout the brain and makes us comprehend things faster.

Have you ever asked a 5-yearold to do something and they are terrible at it? Have you ever asked an adult to do the exact same thing and they do it perfectly? They both have never done the thing that you've asked them to do but the adult has 40 years of neurological pathways connected in their brain and can figure it out. The 5-yearold is just getting started in life and is easily stumped by simple instructions.

If you want to be a better hockey player, be a better soccer player. If you want to understand history better, get better at math. If you want to be smart in literally any area whatsoever of your life, it helps to build neurological pathways in any other area of your brain.

There is no reason you need to ever know how to factor a polynomial or ever need to learn Shakespeare, except for the fact that it builds general brain health. You can learn anything and it makes you smarter and better at totally unrelated topics.

We are forced to learn multiple random unrelated things from kindergarten until we graduate from school. Then, for some reason, we lose motivation and we stop learning. Don't do that.

It does not have to be related to your job whatsoever; just learn something.

You can watch a YouTube series of videos, or a NetFlix documentary, or take an online course. Every single thing you do to make yourself smarter will help you in multiple other areas of your life. Keep learning. Keep it diverse. Learn about plants and flowers. Why? Because your job has nothing to do with plants and flowers. Try to learn a new musical instrument. Why? Because your job has nothing to do with music. The more you learn, the stronger your brain becomes and the better you get at whatever you want to get good at.

SUMMARY: Always be learning new skills and gaining knowledge. It does not have to have anything to do with your job. Learning new things is good for your brain and makes your problem-solving skills increase.

Go Outside

It's ironic that as I write this chapter I am stuck inside on a government-mandated quarantine. There's a worldwide virus right now killing thousands of people and as I write this there is currently no vaccine or proven cure. Because of this, we have all been told to stay inside and only go out if we absolutely have to – groceries and medical visits are pretty much the only reason to see the outside world.

Despite this, I know this will pass. A cure will be developed, a vaccine will be found, and we will eventually get back to our normal lives.

However, many of us will STILL not go outside. We spend far too much time inside. I have a sticker on my desk that I see everyday; it says: "A life outdoors is a life well lived."

I work a job in Corporate America. I spend a lot of time in meetings and behind the screen of a computer, yet I still try to spend time outdoors. Outdoors doesn't even have to be a forest – it can literally be going for a walk in your neighborhood.

I think when this quarantine is over, people are going to appreciate the outside a whole lot more than they used to. However, the memory of the Great COVID Quarantine of 2020 will one day fade. I hope people are still reading my book then and I hope this chapter gives them the kick they need to get outside.

I happen to love parks and wooded areas. Is that not your thing? Fine. You can go outside and still stay downtown. The point is to be out and be active and be experiencing the world. If you are physically able to, get outside.

SUMMARY: *Spend more time outdoors.*

Bookworm Part 2

If you get to the point in your life when you've read a lot of non-fiction books, try adding in fiction.

I personally am a huge fan of non-fiction. Self-help books, business books, and any form of advice book I just eat up. I used to always think that fiction books were a waste of time. Who cares about a made-up story?

Well, there are two types of novels and both are good for you to read.

Type #1 – Novels that make a point

Franz Kafka wrote one of my favorite novels: *The Trial*.

The central point of this book is that bureaucracy is terrible. There are too many rules, too many people to report to, and just simply too many other people. No one knows what's going on, and it's all going to shit.

Kinda a depressing message, right?

The encouraging part is that we can change things. The people who are annoyed at their boss for implementing dumb rules will one day themselves be a boss. When they get into that position, they should remember the pains of being a junior employee and NOT implement those same rules that they hated when it was them.

There are limitless books that make a point that you can dive into. Think George Orwell's *1984*, Ayn Rand's *The Fountainhead*, or Bret Easton Ellis' *American Psycho*.

Regardless of whether or not you or I agree with the central meaning of those three books I just listed off, there are thousands upon thousands of novels that you can dive into that will make you look at the world in a different manner.

Type #2 – Novels that have no point whatsoever

Mark Twain said in the introduction to *The Adventures of Huckleberry Finn* "Persons attempting to find a motive in this narrative will be prosecuted; persons attempting to find a moral in it will be banished; persons attempting to find a plot in it will be shot."

I've read some of Mark Twain's books and I agree with this statement. They are simply rambling stories that have no meaning. They follow Huckleberry Finn and Tom Sawyer as they go on all sorts of adventures. There's no "moral of the story" or lesson learned. It's just two boys being boys.

And that's ok.

Not every book has to have a deeper meaning. Sometimes it's good for your brain to just read a mindless story. It's good for your imagination, it's good for your sense of creativity. Transport yourself to the 1800's in Missouri (where Twain's books take place). Or go to a distant galaxy or read about wizards and witches. It's all good stuff to be reading about.

Just come back to non-fiction when you're done taking a break ;)

SUMMARY: Not every book you read needs to be non-fiction. Read fictional stories that have a moral to teach, and also read fictional stories that are just a good fun read with no deeper meaning.

Expanding Your Knowledge

I used to have a coworker who was a big history buff. He knew everything about World War 1 and 2, the Civil War, various US Presidents, European history including the Greeks and Romans, and Asian history – you name it, this guy seemed to be a walking encyclopedia when it came to history.

One day, two of our younger coworkers were chatting within earshot of Mr. Historybuff and one of them said "Oh hey, have you heard Justin Bieber's newest song? It's so awesome!"

No one was talking to Mr. Historybuff but he decided to butt in: "I wouldn't know who Justin Bieber was if he was standing right in front of me!"

Why is he proud of this? Why is anyone proud of NOT knowing something?

It's perfectly fine if you don't find reality shows interesting, or you only listen to music from the 1970's, or you read books and don't even own a TV – that's fine. But why would you be proud of NOT knowing something? I see this pattern a lot amongst well-educated people thinking it's cool to not know what's going on in today's pop culture, and I also see this pattern amongst people who can name all of the Kardashian sisters who think it's cool to not know anything about world history.

It's not cool. You should be excited to learn things about all of the world, not just your bubble.

Ask yourself if there's an area you know nothing about. You don't have to become an expert in that area, but you also don't have to completely shun the area anytime someone mentions it.

SUMMARY: Broaden your knowledge beyond what you are used to immersing yourself in. Don't be proud of not knowing something or not being interested in certain things. It's ok to have favorites, but it's also always ok to learn new things about subjects you don't care for.

Ronnie Coleman

Ronnie Coleman was a professional bodybuilder who won the Mr. Olympia competition eight times. He was one of the largest bodybuilders to ever live and people's jaws dropped when he would step on the stage and start his posing routine.

One of his famous sayings that has stuck with me is "If you always do what you've always done, you'll always get what you've always got."

Another rendition of this saying is "If it's working, keep doing it, if it's not, change it up."

And, of course, you've heard the original form "If it ain't broke, don't fix it."

Despite these sayings being repeated in common language over and over again, we seem to not heed them. How many times at work is there a new way of doing things when the old way was just fine? Now we have to spend a bunch of time learning the new system and I bet corporate is going to change it again next month.

Well, if you ever get to the spot in your career where you are in charge of changing the system, maybe try to remember back when you were a more junior employee and you hated it when the systems changed. There might not have been much you could have done about it back then, but now you are the big boss man – you have the power to NOT implement this new system. Is the old one working just fine? Then keep it working. No one loves change.

SUMMARY: You only need to change things up when things aren't working. If you're happy with the current results, then keep doing what you're doing. This advice may seem so obvious, but people still don't listen to it.

Pain and Pleasure

I once read in a Tony Robbins book that studies show that people do more to avoid pain than they do to gain pleasure.

Breaking up with someone is hard. It is painful. People will avoid that pain and thus rob themselves of the pleasure of being in a loving and caring and good relationship.

Quitting a job is hard. It is painful. People will avoid that pain and rob themselves of the pleasure of working for a company that mentors them, pays them well, and respects them.

Exercising is hard. It is painful. People will avoid that pain and rob themselves of the pleasure of feeling good about how they look, how they feel, and the extension of life they will have if they had exercised.

This is a sad psychological fact, however you should use it as motivation to finally do that thing you have been putting off. Is there some area of life you want to change but you know it will be painful? Now's the time to finally change. Yes it's going to suck at first. Yes you are going to have false starts and have to try try again. Quitting smoking gives you withdrawals. Quitting drinking or drugs may mean losing a group of friends.

Is it going to be painful? I think it surely will be. Will it be worth it in the end and will you end up gaining more pleasure? I sure hope you will.

SUMMARY: People do more to avoid pain than they do to gain pleasure. Use this fact to convince yourself that you need to go through that painful thing (quitting smoking/drinking/drugs, breaking up with that loser/psycho, quitting that bad job) and you deserve that pleasure that waits at the end of the rainbow.

Buddha

I once travelled to Tibet for a vacation. I wasn't exactly on a deep spiritual quest, rather I was on a vacation where I knew my cellphone wouldn't work and I could finally disconnect from work. It's always good to have some fully-disconnected time.

When in Tibet, I scheduled a number of tours to monasteries. We learned the history of Tibet and the surrounding region as well as some of the overarching principles of Buddhism.

I remember asking our tour guide: "What is the name of the 'Bible' of Buddhism? Do you folks sell it at the gift shop?"

Sadly, it isn't a simple answer. There is no one book that summarizes all of the teachings of Buddhism, probably because the religion has been added to by various Dalai Lamas over the years. He took us into a room in one of the monasteries and it resembled what to me looked like an ancient library. He said "There are 10,000 books in this room. If you read every one of them you will be 1/10,000th of your way to understanding all that Buddhism means."

I understood the theatrics of his answer, so when he was done the tour I took him aside and said "No really…what book should I read?"

He recommended two books:

1) *The Essence of Buddhism* by Traleg Kyabgon
2) *The Heart of The Buddha's Teaching* by Thich Nhat Hanh

NOTE: Thich Nhat Hanh has written many books on a wide range of everyday life subjects and how they relate to Buddhism so if you like book #2, I'd suggest more of Hanh's books.

If you are looking for a quick read, book #1 is fantastic. It goes over all the main tenants of Buddhism including "The Four Noble Truths" and "The Eightfold Noble Path."

Why have I told you all this? Because my next piece of advice is: You should read a book or two (or more) about Buddhism.

Notice how I didn't say "You should become a Buddhist"?

You may be a Christian, a Jew, a Muslim, Agnostic, Atheist, any other religion, or you may fall into the ever-increasing population of "Not-care-ism."

"Not-care-ism" people are those that may have been raised in a particular religion but haven't been to a place of worship in years. They don't hate religion and they don't love it either. There may be a God, there may not be, and they don't really concern themselves with arguing with people about it. Maybe you're in that category.

Whatever category that you are in, books on Buddhism are compatible with your belief system. I can't do them justice by explaining the essentials of Buddhism in a few paragraphs, so I'll stick with my advice "Read a few books on Buddhism." If you follow at least some of the advice it will make you a better Christian, Jew, Muslim, Agnostic, Atheist, or Not-Care-ist. In short: It'll make you a better person.

SUMMARY: Read a couple of books about Buddhism.

Lao Tzu Part 1

In 500 B.C. Chinese mystic Lao Tzu wrote "Tao Te Ching." It is a collection of sayings, proverbs, poems, and advice. One poem that hit me was:

Everyone recognizes beauty only because of ugliness
Allow your life to unfold naturally
Know that it too is a vessel of perfection
Just as you breathe in and breath out
Sometimes you're ahead and other times behind
Sometimes you're strong and other times weak
Sometimes you're with people and other times alone

Life has its ups and downs. We can't win all the time. Life also isn't a zero-sum game. It is possible for some people to win and win and win some more. Karma does not always come and downs do not always come.

You might be down right now. Maybe there's a good reason and maybe you're working to change it. Maybe there's no good reason and you feel down for reasons you can't explain. It might pass, it might not. Lao Tzu said that we can see beauty or we can appreciate the good times when we have seen the ugly or when we've experienced bad times.

Maybe you're going through a bad time right now, or maybe you are going through the best time of your life. I hope it's the latter.

SUMMARY: Remember that we need ups and downs in our lives. No one lives a life that is happiness 24/7.

Lao Tzu Part 2

Lao Tzu once wrote:

The Sage bows to the people
The people bow to the Sage
And when they lift up their heads
*   only greatness remains*

Replace "Sage" with "Boss." How many times can you say that your boss bows down to you? Probably never in a literal sense, but what about in a figurative sense?

Is your boss showing you respect? Is a culture of respect from the top down fostered in your work environment?

Gregg Ward wrote *The Respectful Leader* where he drew on 25 years of leadership that taught him that creating a workplace where people respect one another not only improves productivity, but it is the right and moral thing to do.

You may have a boss who doesn't respect you. Maybe it's time to quit. It's very very tough to get someone to respect you or treat you well. You may have to just walk away. However, you might be a boss or maybe one day you will be a boss. Remember that jerk that you worked for and make a promise to yourself that you will never treat others the way that person treated you. You be the better person.

SUMMARY: Always, in every circumstance, respect one another. If people don't show you respect, you turn the other cheek and you show them even more respect. Know your limit as well and always be ready to walk away and quit.

I know I'm Right

Confirmation Bias is defined as "The tendency to interpret new evidence as confirmation of one's existing beliefs or theories."

A more slick way of saying that would be: "You will always find the evidence for what you choose to believe."

Or another way to say it is: "Studies show that studies will show whatever the hell the author of the study wanted them to show."

Confirmation Bias makes us think that we are right when we may be very very wrong.

On FaceBook we tend to follow pages that are leaning in a certain political direction. Instead of calling it "Conservative" or "Liberal" let's just say "X." You follow X party. X party is followed by celebrities that identify as being X. They post more and more X things. You start to think the whole world must be X and must agree with you. Your mind is blown away when someone from the Y party wins an election. Like, seriously – who the hell voted for that person???

Confirmation Bias can be deadly. You think you aren't sick and you want to convince yourself that everything's ok. Everything might very much not be ok and you might end up dead.

How do you escape Confirmation Bias? How do you know what is "really" going on out in the real world? You watch FoxNews and it says one thing, then you turn on MSNBC and it says literally the exact opposite thing. There are even countless cases of the exact same website saying one thing one day and then the OPPOSITE thing the very next day.

I've found that trying to argue the opposite of what you believe will at least let you see things from other's perspective. Do you have a strong opinion on abortion? Try to argue the opposite. To take it out of the political/social world, do you have a very strong opinion on how the project at work should go? Go through the internal exercise of trying to have an argument with yourself as to why you're wrong.

SUMMARY: Play Devil's Advocate with yourself on a regular basis.

Personal Motto Part 2

When I was in middle school one of my teachers challenged us to come up with a personal motto, translate it into Latin, then make a family crest that had the motto on it – similar to the American "Great Seal of the United States" that has an eagle clutching arrows with the Latin saying "E pluribus unum" meaning "Out of many, one."

Coming up with a cool crest design and a saying was pretty straight forward…translating it into Latin was something my teacher didn't think through.

We completed this middle school assignment before the internet age and Latin has been a dead language for almost 1,300 years, so our teacher pivoted and said we should use the English-to-Italian dictionary that we had in the school library and that would be "close enough."

My saying was "Always think of the consequences" and I mis-translated it as "Sempre pensa del conseguenze." Now, many years later, I've finally put it into a Google translator and see that I should have put "Pensa sempre alle conseguenze." And seeing as how I'm right here with a translator that will do every language known to man, I can now put in "Latin" and see what I should have said: Semper congitare de consequatur.

Neat.

Anyways, the point is that I wanted to think of the consequences of my actions. From a young middle school age I was trying to set Future Grant up for success. What could I do that might be a bit painful or annoying now but will pay off big in the future?

Exercise comes to mind. Forget about "quitting" drinking or smoking – I was 14 years old. I hadn't even started these things and I never did. How about starting to save up money each month? How about starting to study for the SATs? Why wait until senior year?

Whatever point you are at in your life, you can't change the past. However, you can start to plan for the future. Are you in your 40's? That's fine. Plan for your 50's. Are you in your 80's? Great. You can start planning for your 100th birthday.

The overarching point is that we probably have a lot of life left to live and if we start doing things now, and slowly chip away at them, eventually it will/may come back to pay big dividends.

SUMMARY: Always think of the consequences. Start planning now for the 1, 5, and 10 years from now version of you.

Happiness

First off, I can't do this topic justice in one short chapter. I would suggest further reading of books like *Joy, Inc.* by Richard Sheridan, *If you're so smart, why aren't you happy* by Raj Raghunathan, *The Happiness Advantage* by Shawn Anchor, and *Rest* by Alex Soojung-Kim Pang.

The central theme of all those books is:

"Success does not bring happiness – Happiness brings success."

There are many things you can do to make yourself happier. There are tips and tricks you can follow. I hope a lot of them you find in the book you are currently holding. However, there are also a lot of outside factors that are out of your control. Maybe you have to quit your job to get away from a bad boss. But maybe you can't quit. Maybe you are suffering from an illness or you have depression. These problems can persist your whole life and I can't pretend I have a magic bullet to fix them.

All I can say is that admitting there's a problem is the first step, and legitimately looking for a solution is the second step.

Books help. Going to see a licensed professional helps. Heck, even talking it through with a friend helps. Sometimes people just "snap out of it." Have you ever met someone who is going through a really tough time and yet they have a smile on their face? Conversely, have you ever personally known someone or known of a famous person who seemingly "had it all" and yet they killed themselves?

The human brain is extremely complicated and I can't begin to say I fully understand it, but what I can say is that through reading, listening, asking questions, and going on a journey to try to find happiness, it can be found. There will be ups and downs, but you can get to a world of happiness eventually and then you can create your own definition of what success is.

SUMMARY: Remember that success does not bring happiness – happiness brings success.

Ayn Rand

Ayn Rand was a Russian-born author who is most famous for her novels *Atlas Shrugged*, and *The Fountainhead*.

Her works have been translated into multiple languages, and because of this one quote of hers she is often praised as being a hero of the American Republican Party: "Those who deny individual rights cannot claim to be defenders of minorities."

Both her books are huge and difficult for most to read. Because of that, most don't read them and simply assume what they say.

I read *The Fountainhead* and either I missed the point completely, or I did get the point and I disagree with it entirely.

The book is centered on two architects – Howard Roark and Peter Keating. Peter is the kind of guy that listens to his clients and does what they ask. They want a lobby full of gold trim and plants? Well then that's what they're going to get. Do they want vaulted ceilings in the apartments? Then he'll design them that way.

One the other hand, Howard meets with clients and immediately tells them to shut up and that they don't know what they are talking about.

The central point of the novel is that we should be like Howard. We should have principles, stick to them, and not let anyone persuade us otherwise.

I understand having principles that you want to stick to, but the Howard character takes things to an absurd level. We need to be a bit of Howard and a bit of Peter. Yes, have lines you won't cross, but also don't be a jerk about it. I see this all too often in society that people are completely unwilling to make even the smallest compromise. You may be right, but you're being a jerk about it. Don't be a jerk.

SUMMARY: Don't be a jerk. It's ok to have your principles and your lines that you won't cross, but you don't have to be annoying or rude or a jerk about it. Let's all try to be more polite and respectful to one another.

Giving Back

I've said it in other places in this book and I'll saying it again: Chances are, that if you're reading this book, you are probably already pretty successful.

Maybe you've got a six-figure income, maybe you're in great physical shape, maybe you're an upper level manager, maybe you have a job you love and makes you happy, or maybe you're in a great relationship.

I hope this is the case. If it isn't, I hope this book will help you get there.

Regardless of where you're at, it may be time to start to think about giving back.

I'm going to assume that you're in a good place, so I'll use this opportunity to encourage you to give to charity, start to volunteer, or maybe do something as simple as call one of your relatives that you don't talk to very often and just let them know that you are thinking about them.

The number of ways you can give back is endless. I can't even begin to list them all off.

Do I personally fall short of my own goals of giving back? Yes, yes I do. I would say that of all the pieces of advice in this book, "Giving Back" is probably the area where I personally could do a much better job in.

So let's make the pledge today, together, to each find a way that we can give back.

It can be small, it can be big, or somewhere in between.

We are blessed with the life that we live – let's find a way to give back.

SUMMARY: Find ways to give back. Charity, volunteer work, or even just calling a relative. Let's make the world a better place.

Section Two:
Career Building

Networking

A great way to advance in your career is to join an association that meets regularly in-person.

There are countless numbers of "Young Professional" groups that you can join if you are just starting out your career.

If you have 5-10 years of experience, it may be time to join other associations. If you're above the 10 year mark, you should start to think about joining a committee that decides rules and regulations for your industry.

By joining an association you will network and make contacts all across your industry. You shouldn't be planning on leaving your job on a regular basis, but layoffs do happen and sometimes we can't escape a down-sizing. Therefore, having several contacts throughout your industry is a fantastic idea.

If job security doesn't interest you, how about rising the corporate ladder? By being on a committee, you are at the forefront of your industry. You will have sway over the rules and regulations that govern your industry.

If you were a boss, would you give that person a promotion or at least treat them well? I know I sure would.

SUMMARY: Join several associations and/or committees. It will help you network so you have job security, and it will improve your standing at your own company.

VIPs

Throughout your career, you are going to meet people at your company that are big shots. If you work for a small firm, you might see them on a regular basis. If you work for a giant firm, you might never meet the top dogs.

When you do meet someone who is high up the corporate ladder, use the opportunity to maybe gain a mentor. You can't just ask someone "Will you be my mentor?" This will come off as forced and awkward.

Many big shots love talking about themselves. In fact, many people who aren't big shots love talking about themselves. So ask them questions about how long they've been with the company, how they got their start, and what they are currently up to.

A mentor is not going to automatically start mentoring you – you need to first show that you can be of assistance to them.

You've got your skills and they've got their projects. Do any of their projects overlap with your skills? Use the opportunity to follow up with them a few days or weeks later to ask if you could be involved in one of their projects and help out.

You are going to first have to prove to them that you are a useful employee before they start to mentor you.

Keep a list of the important people in your company. Reach out to them on a regular basis. Not too regular as to appear annoying, but make sure they know that you are keen and wanting to help out. Eventually they might find a need that you can fill and you will be the first person they call.

You might have to work for them for a while before they start to mentor you. They might never mentor you, but put in the effort to help them first, and it has a high likelihood of paying off massive dividends in the long run.

SUMMARY: Create a list of "big shots" that you've met in the company and reach out to them to see if you can be on their team and help them. Eventually, they will become a mentor and help you in return.

Career Arc

Do you know someone at work who has been with the company for 40 years and yet still sits in the exact same cubicle as they did when they first graduated from college? Maybe that is your dream, but it certainly wasn't mine.

I have tried to break my career up into 5-year chunks. Anything shorter can be a recipe for disaster, and anything longer can make you depressed that things aren't progressing.

I spent the first 5 years of my career working on the ground floor. For me, that was construction. I worked in house renovations, new home construction, concrete pouring and rebar placing, and building inspection.

For the next 5 years, I was in university, studying to become an engineer.

After the marriage of real-life experience in construction and a 5-year engineering degree, I was able to land a job at the company that I still work at to this day.

Now what should you do for the next 5 years? Well, the first 5 years of your career should be spent soaking up as much knowledge and experience as you can.

I worked for many different project managers and bosses and worked across the corporation in multiple disciplines. This is how you network and how you grow. This is also how you figure out what you are good at and what drives you nuts.

If you are in the beginning of your career, make sure you aren't pigeon-holed into doing just one thing. You need to have variety otherwise you'll never grow. Don't become known as the guy that is constantly getting bored either. You need to stick with a position for months before you ask for a new challenge...but don't wait years.

The next 5 years of your career should be spent on mastering the small group of things that you are awesome at. You may be awesome at 6 things, but pick 3 of them and hit them out of the park. You can't be a jack of all trades and expect to actually be good at all of the trades.

These 5 years should be spent growing your skills in a small area and showing that you can lead teams and manage projects. You're still young, but you are ambitious and focused.

Now you've reached the 10-year mark. Now it's time to really soar. A 10-year employee (depending on the industry) is getting into the six-figure salaries. You should be getting not only invited to important meetings, but you should be actively contributing. A 10-15 year employee has the makings of a junior executive and this is your time to shine.

Years 15-20 can feel an awful lot like years 10-15, depending on your company. Maybe it's time to change to a new company. Studies show that the most common time to leave a company and take a giant promotion at a competitor is at the 15 year mark. Good managers will recognize this and promote you. Bad managers won't care...so maybe you should pursue options at a different firm.

Years 20-30 might be another time to soar, or you may have found your happy place. Many people get to the spot in their career that they love and they have no desire to advance any further. That's great. If you are happy, then you are winning.

Most CEOs in America become CEO around their 25-30 year anniversary with the industry. They are long enough in that they know what they are talking about, but not too old so that retirement is right around the corner. If you've hit your 30-year anniversary, wherever you are at is probably close to where you are going to get to within the corporate structure.

At 40 years, it's generally time to either retire, or take a few steps back. One of my original bosses retired at their 39th work anniversary and went to work driving a food delivery truck for the local food bank. It keeps him active and he enjoys helping people.

There's life after retirement, and 40 years in the business is a great time to cash out.

SUMMARY: Break your career up into 5-year chunks. Every 5 years it's time for a big move...hopefully upwards, but maybe laterally.

Awards & Thankyous

Do you work hard? Of course you do. Does your coworker also work hard? Well, you might not like them or get along with them, but sometimes you have to admit that they also work hard as well. Then guess what happens: The boss comes over and gives a big thank you to your coworker and doesn't say a word to you.

How do you feel?

You feel like crap. You worked just as hard if not harder than they did, yet they got all the praise and you got nothing.

This is a problem that you might not be able to solve. How do you go to your boss and say "Um, excuse me. Why didn't you also thank me?"

That's not going to go over well.

Instead, what you can do, is turn the situation around. You have a team that you work with. You might not have people that report to you, as you might not be a manager or a boss, but you at least should have some people that you are with on a regular basis.

Thank them. Thank every single one of them. Don't leave anyone out.

You got slighted and feel bad because you weren't thanked or praised, so instead of seeking thanks, go and give thanks to others.

Keep being a positive influence around your company, and eventually you'll get the thanks or recognition that you deserve. If you don't, go work for the competitor.

SUMMARY: Thank your team members and coworkers. Bring positivity to the group even when others bring negativity. If the negativity or lack of praise continues, go work for a different company.

Cashing Out

Is there a boss at work that you can't stand or a process that you are told to follow that makes no sense at all? Throughout my career, I've worked for many Project Managers and bosses. I've had many clients. For the most part, they have all been great. Any disputes or differences have been talked about, resolved, and managed. But occasionally a client comes along or a new boss comes along that just simply cannot be worked with.

What do you do?

Well, first of all you try all the tips and tricks in this book. You might want to read *Working with Difficult People* by Amy Cooper Hakim. She lays out the ten types of problem people that you are likely to run into in Corporate America. Her helpful tips have helped me navigate some particularly terrible clients and bosses.

However, sometimes you must cash out.

I've had clients that were so unreasonable in their requests (or demands) that we as a team made the decision to walk away. That's why it's a good idea to invoice on a regular basis, and not wait until the project is over. Monthly invoicing is a very good idea.

Maybe you've had a boss that was awful to work with. You can try moving to a different division within the company, but if they are inescapable, it may be time to move to one of your competitors.

SUMMARY: Try to work with the jerks in your life, whether they be clients or coworkers. However, you may need to eventually say goodbye to a client or quit your job if things never get better.

Getting Kicked

Let's pretend that you've spent the last two months working on that big project. You've gone over it again and again, checking with everyone on the team. You've done revision after revision and made so many changes you lost count. You eat, sleep, and breath this project and now it's finally the big day – you are presenting it to the client.

You put on your best clothes, print off all the documents, and make sure to show up 30 minutes early to the meeting just so you are there and ready.

You walk into the client's boardroom and set up the presentation that is going to showcase your masterpiece.

And you wait.

And you continue to wait.

Eventually, the client shows up, 10 minutes late, on their phone, no apology for being late. You start your presentation. You finish your presentation.

Silence.

The client finally says "Well…um…that was ok. I was thinking we'd doing something a bit different though. I'm not quite sure what's wrong with it, but I'll think about it and let you know. Thanks for coming in."

And with that, the client gets up and leaves.

Their feedback was pretty much useless to you. You and your team worked your ass off for months and the feedback that you got wasn't going to help you at all.

You feel like crap.

This used to happen to teams of mine on a regular basis. I remember one time we spent months designing bridges that were going to be built in a park. The challenge of this project was that the final location of the pathway through the park had not been decided upon. This means that if the path moves a hundred feet to the west the river that it was crossing is now much larger and thus the bridge needs to be longer. Or if it moves to the east the two rivers had not yet merged so now instead of one large river, the path was crossing two smaller rivers. Finally, if the path moved to the other side of the valley, the soil conditions would be different, so the foundations of the bridges would be different.

My design team was faced with this challenge: How do you design a series of bridges when you do not know how many bridges you need to design, you don't know their length, and you aren't sure of what types of foundations they will require?

The solution to this conundrum was to make a "Lego-Style" bridge system.

We designed 5-foot panels that could snap together to create bridges that were 5, 10, 15, 20 or any multiple of 5 foot lengths.

The foundations were precast concrete blocks with 8" holes predrilled into them. If the soil was hard, we would place the blocks on a gravel pad and build the bridge. If the soil was a bit soft we would drive piles through some of the holes in the blocks. If the soil was really soft, we would fill all the holes with piles.

We designed the entire system as a Lego-block snap-together system so literally all we had to do was pick from a table to create whatever bridge the client wanted. We were incredibly proud of this project.

We went to one meeting and after presenting it to the client the only piece of feedback that we got was "Can you make the bridges horse-colored?"

Horse-colored?

Yes, he was serious. He wanted the bridge to be the color of horses.

I said "We'll research various add-mixtures that we can put into the concrete and show you a few varieties then you can pick which color you like the most."

That was the end of the meeting. No other comments or notes were given.

The team spent months designing a set of bridges with no predetermined length, location, or soil conditions, and instead of winning the Nobel Prize in "Designing something that has no preset specifications" we were told to change the color.

We should have seen this coming. This sort of feedback was pretty common from some of the members on this client's team.

In the early stages of the project, when we were presenting conceptual designs and possible locations of the pathway, the headers and footers and general color-theme of the documents we presented was blue.

It was blue because the logo of the company that I was working for was blue and blue is a pretty common color in engineering. Plus, it looks nice. Currently as I'm writing this I realize that I'm wearing a blue shirt. Blue is a perfectly reasonable color to wear and also to put into your headers and footers.

We spent months creating this massive document full of drawings and sketches and printed off reems of paper.

We got one piece of feedback: Can you make the color scheme less blue? Can you make it red instead?

You see, when we started the project, a certain political party was funding the project. (This project didn't take place in America, so you aren't correct in assuming Blue means Democrat and Red means Republican – it's also not relevant to the story). The political party at the beginning of the project was traditionally blue, but during the project an election happened and now a political party whose colors were red was in charge. Their only feedback on the giant report was to change the color-scheme to red.

Not only is this a pointless, petty task, it is a fairly labor-intensive task. The entire document may be presented nicely in one 4" binder…but it is made up of hundreds of separate PDFs, Word Documents, drawings, sketches, Excel print outs and various other files that will now have to be edited one at a time.

What a complete waste of time.

But that is par for the course when you work in Corporate America. The budgets on giant infrastructure projects are enormous. The price of a bridge or a stadium or a hospital or a new highway is in the billions of dollars.

Why? Because of stupid things like changing the color. Study after study is created only to be never read and put on a shelf.

It's a bigger problem outside of the purview of this book that we have in society with the uselessness of some jobs and the wasted time in Corporate America. I'm not going to try to fix it in this chapter. What I am trying to point out is that this is the world that we live in and we have to work with it.

You are going to have clients that do not care one bit about the actual product and just want the color scheme their way. Or they are about to get a promotion into a different division so it really doesn't matter what you present – the new guy is going to have to deal with it and they don't want to rock the boat before they leave. Or maybe it's their job to point out problems. Even if there is not a problem, they have to point something out, otherwise they lose their job.

So get used to it – you are going to have clients who don't appreciate anything that you do. They are still going to pay your invoices and they might continue to give you work over and over again. I must say that the two clients I've been talking about throughout this chapter have paid us a lot of money throughout the years and many of the interactions that we've had with them have been excellent. Many of the people at their office are really nice people and they give us a lot of great feedback. However, we tend to remember that one guy at the meeting who was focused on the wrong thing.

Clients will sometimes be appreciative of what you do for them, and sometimes they really won't seem to care. That's life, and you are going to have to prepare yourself to get used to it.

SUMMARY: Your great idea is not always going to be celebrated by others. You need to develop a thick skin and become fantastic at getting kicked during a meeting.

Strengths & Weaknesses Part 1

Have you ever met someone who is terrible at something, yet they keep trying to tell people how good they are at that exact thing? In the worst case, you might have had a boss who is terrible at something but tries to tell the whole office how to do it. Sometimes employees will agree with the boss to their face, then once they've left the room they'll all agree they aren't going to do it that way.

I've written a chapter on "Cashing out" that gives the advice that sometimes you might have to quit a company to escape a bad boss. This chapter seeks to turn the problem around and asks you: Is there something that you are terrible at but you keep trying to push it at work?

Stop doing that.

I've interviewed a number of new graduates and I've asked them the question "Where do you see yourself in 5 or 10 years?" Many of them reply by saying "Project Management or General Management."

That is a fine answer, but I suspect that they might be chasing the money.

My standard reply is "That's a good goal. Did you know that our drafters and designers actually make more money than our management team?"

They pause, then they say "Well, I really like drafting and design as well."

I then say "Drafters and designers don't make more money than management. I think you just want to do the job that makes the most amount of money."

I don't fault young college graduates for being caught up in the money trap. Of course they want to make money. The point I'm trying to make to them is that we shouldn't chase a job just because it makes more money. We should instead find the things that we are good at and do those things. We need to play to our strengths.

There's a term in Corporate America called "The Peter Principle." It was developed by Laurence J. Peter and he noticed that people who work in a hierarchal system tend to continue to get promoted until they get to a level of incompetence. This is because the skills that made them do an awesome job at the entry level job do not necessarily translate up the corporate ladder.

If you are really good at cleaning toilets does that mean you should be the manager of the cleaning staff? The manager of the cleaning staff needs to check inventory of cleaning supplies, order new items when stock is running low, check in with people's schedules to make sure we have enough staff on site when peak usage is occurring, and deal with interpersonal issues when one cleaner doesn't want to work with another, etc.

Do any of those tasks have anything to do with the physical act of cleaning a toilet?

Now, I'm not saying that if you are at one level you can't rise to the next; that is pretty much how all promotions occur. What I'm saying is that just because you were good at the thing you were doing it does not mean you will instantly be good at the next level up.

We all have weaknesses. We can all work on them.

I've written a chapter on how to clean things, both literally and figuratively, and the advice of that chapter is to clean from cleanest thing to dirtiest thing. This advice applies well when trying to strengthen one of your weaknesses.

Are there one or two things at work that you are pretty good at, but still need some practice to get better at? Good – work on those things. Is there something that you are absolutely terrible at? Well, maybe let that one go, at least for now.

We all have weaknesses that can be strengthened, but don't kill yourself trying to be good at something that you will never ever be good at. You have to know when to walk away.

SUMMARY: Play to your strengths. Find the area you are good at and a job that fits those skill sets. Strengthen your weaknesses, but realize that some things you will never be good at. Strengthen those things that are manageable and fixable.

Strengths & Weaknesses Part 2

One of my most-admired mentors has a doctorate. On car rides to jobsites or meetings, or in the lunchroom, him and I have spent countless hours discussing business and how to make things better. He's responsible for a fair bit of the advice in this book.

One item we have discussed is the strength and also the weakness of having a Ph.D.

His resume and his business card clearly show his doctorate. He is a world-renowned expert on bridges, specializing in suspension and cable-stayed bridges – think Golden Gate Bridge type structures.

However, he usually signs his emails with simply his first name. He oftentimes leaves out all the letters he has after his last name.

Why?

Because sometimes when you are emailing someone and you put "Ph.D" behind your name, your strength becomes your weakness.

He learned early on in his career that people would see that doctorate and immediately groan. "Oh man, this guy is going to turn the project into a science experiment! I don't want to work with this guy!" was the feedback he was getting.

Many people who have doctorates in their field are brilliant and have a genius way of simplifying complex subjects down so anyone can understand them. He was in this category.

Unfortunately, there are enough people who have doctorates who are terrible communicators and have a bad attitude that they ruin it for the entire community.

For this reason, he does not lead with his credentials. He lets the actual words that are coming out of his mouth speak for themselves.

Have you ever been in a meeting where someone says "I went to school for this and I'm an expert in this area"? That's great. Then what's the answer to our problem?

The room is going to be far more receptive to someone saying "I think we should consider doing it this way. I've tried that on previous jobs and it worked."

Proven results are far more impressive than letters behind your name or certificates up on your wall.

Smart people realize this. They realize that their "strength" – the doctorate – actually becomes their weakness. Therefore, they downplay it, or don't mention it at all. They let their proven track record do the talking.

That is the first part of this chapter: My strength is my weakness.

The second part may be hard to comprehend if English is your second language, but here goes: My strength is my weakness.

What? Didn't I just write the same sentence again? Yes I did, but this time it means something completely different.

For a full discussion of this phenomenon, check out Malcolm Gladwell's best-selling book *David and Goliath*. He goes into far more detail than the next few paragraphs that I'll use to summarize the same message.

Do you think that having a stutter would make you a good public speaker? The obvious answer is no. Is a lawyer required to be a good public speaker if they are to win a case in court? The obvious answer is yes. However, Gladwell shows that many lawyers who have speech impediments actually win more cases. That is because people root for the underdog and a lawyer who trips over their words a bit comes off as more genuine that a smooth-talking lawyer.

Would someone with dyslexia be good with numbers and destined to become a billionaire? Your immediate gut reaction is no. However, Richard Branson, the billionaire founder of over 400 companies has famously stated that he is terrible with numbers. That is why he has to pour over them very carefully.

The basic summary of Gladwell's book is that that thing that you may consider a weakness can actually be played to your advantage and become your strength.

SUMMARY: Your strength is your weakness: Impressing people with your certificates (your strength) can make you look like a show-off and people won't want to work with you. Lead with solutions to the problem, not self-congratulations. Your strength is your weakness: If you have a weakness (a stutter, dyslexia, shyness) you can use it to your advantage. Read Malcolm Gladwell's "David and Goliath" for a full discussion of how to do this.

Stages

I used to see only junior employees make this mistake but the more I've worked as a *Project Management Analyst* the more I've seen senior employees make this mistake as well:

Make sure to check the stages, don't just check the final product.

Whatever it is that we are working on, there are various steps and milestones that we get to that we can show to our boss to see if we are on the right track. Waiting until the project is completely done to then show them is a dangerous game to play. You may have missed the mark by a long shot and wasted a bunch of time.

Of course, there are some problems that you might not be able to avoid.

I once worked on a multi-month project where I sent update emails to my boss every week. He worked in a different city and email was the only way to contact him. I was leading a team of engineers and I made sure that every Friday I sent him the latest calculations, reports, and all other deliverables we were working on, regardless of if they were done or not. I wanted him to see where we were at each Friday.

Each Monday I would get a response. It was always the same. "Looks good – thanks."

This went on for months.

When the project was finally done, I sent the complete package to him. It was only then that it was revealed to me that he had not been looking at any of the attachments – he had just been replying with "Looks good – thanks."

This wasn't the first time in my career this happened. It wasn't common, but people saying "I love it" when they haven't even looked at it is a problem more common than you would suspect. My advice in this regard is to call them up and point blank say: "Did you actually look at it?" This is tricky, as it can come off as rude. A better way to phrase the same question would be to say "Can you look at page 5? I wasn't sure which one you wanted me to do. Can you look at both options and tell me what you think?" This will force them to at least open the attachments.

Another point about stage-checking that I want to bring up is: What happens when you have a brand-new idea? Do you bring everyone on board at the beginning of the project and get input all the way throughout? Or do you do the complete project in secret and make a big reveal at the end? Both options have pitfalls.

A coworker of mine once had a big idea for a new technology that we should invest into. He literally spent thousands of his own dollars to buy new equipment, license the software, get the governmental approvals, and do this all in secret. When it was all done, he proudly walked into his boss's office and showed off the new technology.

His boss was annoyed. He almost got fired.

The problem here was that he was working for a boss who wanted to be involved in all the steps. He didn't like people doing things without his knowledge. My coworker should have involved his boss from the very beginning.

The other alternative is to involve everyone. This has its drawbacks as well. When you involve everyone, everyone has their own special opinion and it slows the process right down. Sometimes, it even kills the entire idea.

Knowing which types of bosses you work for, who to bring onto the team, and to what level you are willing to bend the rules is unique to your team. It's going to take some trial and error to figure it out for your situation.

SUMMARY: When working on a big project, get yes/no from your boss at multiple stages and don't wait for the final product to get a review. Make sure they are actually looking at it and opening your PDF attachment. When you want to create a big change at work, weigh the benefits of keeping everything a secret vs. involving everyone. Think about the personalities that you work for and answer the question: Would they be pissed off if I did this in secret? Or would they be impressed?

Massive Frustration

Tony Robbins once said "The key to success is massive frustration."

If you can walk into a place of business, apply, get interviewed, get trained, and start working all in the same day, chances are you won't be making much more than minimum wage.

You didn't have any frustration in the job-search…but you probably won't have a lot of financial success at this place either.

If you had to write a proposal as to what your vision was for the company, you had 12 phone call interviews, 4 in-person interviews, and you had to fly all over the country to meet with various people before you finally got your job, chances are you are going to have a lot of financial success at this place.

That is the trade off. When things are easy, there generally isn't a lot of reward at the end of them. When things are hard, there's a good chance it's going to be great when it's done.

Are you going through a hard time trying to get your new initiative approved by the big bosses? Well, it's probably a pretty big idea and needs to be thought about a lot. Keep your head up. It might just turn out great for you.

Was that other thing you asked for granted with no pushback whatsoever? Well, then there's a possibility that it's not all that great.

Of course, there's instances when something is easy and a huge success. There's cases when things are hard and they are still lame. The point I'm trying to make is that you need to step back an evaluate what situation you are in. Are you certain this is a great idea but you are frustrated at how long it's taking to implement? Good – keep going. It will be worth it in the end.

SUMMARY: Remember that massive success usually does not come without massive frustration.

Forbes

Since 1982 Forbes magazine has been publishing the list of the 400 wealthiest American Citizens. When the list first started, there were only 13 billionaires on it, and if you had a net worth of $91 million or higher you made the list. Since 2004, only people with a net worth over a billion dollars have made the list. In 2019, there were 221 billionaires in America that didn't make the list. $2.1 billion is the new bar for how "poor" you need to be to NOT make the list.

Is your goal to make this list? That's a pretty huge goal, but it is attainable. You're probably going to have to start a business that is the "Next big thing" or you are going to have to be incredibly lucky in the stock market. Still, it is possible for whoever is reading this book to one day make the Forbes list. When you woke up this morning, was your name on the Forbes list? No? Well then keep working at it.

Having a goal that is monumental can be a good motivator for people. Is your goal to get in shape? Then set a goal of running a marathon. You might never actually run a marathon, but if your goal is to run 100 yards, you might not do that either. Setting huge goals and working towards them is a great way to get something accomplished, even if you don't come close to the actual goal.

You've probably heard the expression "Shoot for the moon – if you miss you'll end up in the stars" or "You have to think, so why not THINK BIG?"

There are lots of things that can give us motivation – shooting for a supremely high goal is one way of at least getting something accomplished, even if it's only a sliver of the original goal. It's better than sitting on your couch and doing nothing.

SUMMARY: Set HUGE goals. Come up with a plan for how to get there. You will most likely fail to hit your original goal – climbing Mount Everest, becoming a billionaire, or being President – but you will most likely succeed in getting in better shape, making more money, or getting elected to local office.

Fruit

We go through stages in our career. When we first graduate, hopefully we are at a company that has lots of good mentors and leaders. Hopefully we are in a good headspace where we want to learn and become better at our job.

As we continue to work at the company, we hopefully get promoted. Maybe it's an actual pay raise and change in title, or maybe it's simply our boss getting us to do a task that we didn't know how to do. Either way, we always naturally tend to get better at our job.

The problem we may face though is stagnation. We sometimes get to a point when we don't want to learn any more things, we don't want to take on any more responsibility, and we want to just stay where we are comfortable.

An old saying that a former boss said to me comes to mind:

"When we're green we grow. When we ripen we rot."

When we are 22 years old and young and eager, it's easy to grow. The challenge becomes when we are 33 or 44 or 55. It's pretty darn easy to be ripe by that age, and that's when we start to rot.

This can happen at any age and at any time throughout our career. It can and will happen multiple times. It's ok to be in a funk. It's ok to not want to push yourself. What's not ok is to stay in that funk forever.

Take some time, take a break for a bit, but eventually you have to get back on that horse. A new skill, a new job, a new task, or literally anything that you will be green at.

SUMMARY: When you're green you grow, when you ripen you rot. Make sure to keep pushing yourself to learn new things and develop your skills. Don't stay in your rut forever.

Easing in and Out

How many times do we get emails from Corporate that are announcing a BIG CHANGE! There's a new way of doing things around here and everyone is going to change instantly.

Except we don't.

When change is big, resistance to change is big as well. We have new initiatives launched seemingly on a monthly basis and still no one gets the message. I once heard a coworker say "Why should I bother learning the new system? They are just going to change it next month anyways."

When change is large, it's unlikely that it will be adhered to. That is why corporations need to learn to take baby steps when implementing a change. Phased approaches to new software, new processes, new systems, or new techniques, is the only way that humans will adapt. We figure out small things – we hate big changes.

Similarly, how do you personally approach a big change that you want to make in your career?

Maybe you are tired of being a drafter. You want to become a designer. Can you march into your boss's office and demand that you become a designer? Go ahead and try it. You'll probably fail.

Instead, you need to ease into it. You should start with a casual conversation. Then you should have another casual conversation. Then you should email your boss about it. Continuing to ask what needs to be done to transition into becoming a designer is something you're going to need to chip away at and keep easing into. Similarly, how do you stop being a drafter? It's the same technique, just in reverse. You need to ease out of it.

Is there that big job coming up that you were going to be in charge of? Maybe you work in more of a supporting roll as you are transitioning out of being a drafter.

Whatever the role is that you don't want to be in anymore, and whatever the role is that you want to be in, I would suggest a slow ease-out, ease-in approach. This helps everyone adjust and doesn't leave anyone hanging.

Changing roles is one thing. But what about changing up how you operate in your current role?

Use the same technique. If you have been working 9-5, Monday-Friday and you want to start working from home on Friday, it will be noticed if suddenly you're gone. Talk it over with your boss and see if you can work a half day on Friday once a month. Then twice a month. Then every week. Pretty soon, you're working from home every Friday. The people who go cold-turkey Fridays off are the people who will annoy their coworkers. "Hey, where's Bob? I needed to talk to him!" will be a problem if you didn't ease into it.

Retirement falls into this category as well. One of my best mentors of all time gave a 5-year warning about his retirement. He groomed the team for him leaving. In his final year, he acted as a junior employee, allowing his replacements to tell him what to do, so that he knew that they knew what they were doing. He eased into retirement in the best way possible.

SUMMARY: Whether it's a change in a company-wide system, a job promotion, retirement, or simply a way that you do your day-to-day work, make sure to ease into it. This gives your coworkers time to adjust and if done properly, people won't even notice it or complain at all.

Bridge Burning

Never burn a bridge.

Never ever ever burn a bridge.

My cousin worked a job once for a mean boss. This guy was a real jerk, and when he quit he really wanted to tell this guy off. But he didn't. The rage that you will feel when you want to blow up at someone will pass. The bridge that you burnt will always be burnt.

My cousin went on to work at a different company and when it was time for a promotion, they called up his old company. He got a glowing review and got the promotion.

Sometimes these types of stories never happen. You had a jerk of a boss, you didn't burn a bridge, and it never came back to you in a positive or negative way. Who cares? You need to let it go. Never burn a bridge.

I've had bosses that I did not like. When I transferred to another division or went to work for another company, I sent them a nice thank you email. Never burn a bridge.

A lot of people think that you shouldn't burn a bridge because you may need to cross it some time in the future. That is not why you shouldn't burn bridges. You shouldn't burn bridges because burning a bridge is wrong. Be a good person, not a bad person. It doesn't matter if you will never see that person ever again. It doesn't matter if they will never ever be in a position to help you ever again.

Be a good person and never ever ever burn a bridge.

Got it?

SUMMARY: No matter how hard it may be to keep your cool, never ever ever burn a bridge. End on a high note in every situation. It doesn't matter if it will never come back to haunt you; that's not the point. Be a good person, not a bad person. Never burn a bridge.

Writing

You spend a lot of your day writing emails and/or texting. If you don't, you probably spend a lot of your day talking. You have a lot of ideas and opinions.

You should start writing them down.

If you work in a highly technical field, maybe it's time for you to write a paper or an article and submit it to an industry journal. The doors this could open for you at work could be massive.

Or maybe it could start with something simple like writing a blog post to you company's internal social media page.

Some people start an office newsletter. Some people write update emails to their families. Did you write a Christmas letter last year? Maybe this is the year to write one.

Or how about writing a book? You have a lot of ideas and stories you want to share with the world. You also have a laptop. Start writing them down. Who cares if they never get published or no one but you reads them? Do you think the first thing that any of the New York Times bestsellers wrote ended up published? Of course not. They wrote for years in obscurity.

Writing is a healthy thing to do. It helps you collect your thoughts, it builds your typing skills, and it is a distraction from the rest of the world. Do yourself a favor and start writing a paper/article/novel/book.

SUMMARY: Attempt to write a book or an article or a paper. It'll be a fantastic experience even if it never gets off the ground and you are the only person that reads it. Just give it a try.

Pivot!

I had a coworker who wanted to make drone videos for government clients. He spent $10,000 buying all the drone equipment and tried to sell his services to big clients.

No one took him up on his offer.

He then bought a little bit more camera equipment and started shooting weddings.

He started to make money and made back his original investment.

He got into website design. He tried to build websites for others...that went nowhere.

He moved back to his hometown and ran into an old friend of his. His friend had a mobile cellphone repair company. He said "Let me shoot a commercial for you."

He used his drone to shoot a cool flyover of the van, his camera gear to create a neat video, and they then packaged it together and auditioned to be on TV's hit show "Shark Tank."

They got on the show and got to meet all the Sharks. I remember smiling ear-to-ear when I saw my former coworker on primetime TV.

Did his dream of being a drone pilot ever pan out? No it did not. Did he go far beyond his wildest dreams and get to be on Shark Tank? Yes he did.

The key was his ability to pivot. Take one set of skills from one area and move them into a new area. Let things build on each other. Don't be discouraged when one thing doesn't work out. Use what you learned in the first job to expand on what you are doing in the next job.

SUMMARY: Pivot your skillsets. You are good at X, so use it to help you out doing Y.

Celebrated

Don't stay where you're tolerated, go where you're celebrated.

As I write this we are in the middle of a worldwide health crisis. A deadly virus, COVID-19, is killing thousands and by the time this is all over it may kill millions. Further to that, it's not even calculatable how many people have lost their jobs because almost every single person is "working from home" which in many accounts means they aren't working very much.

Despite the massive layoffs all across the world, I have a friend who is thinking about quitting and going to work for a competitor.

His boss definitely does not celebrate him. His boss tolerates him, and that's not the environment anyone wants to be in.

It's ok to get some pushback here and there, but when you feel like everything you do is second-guessed and it's a struggle to do anything, then maybe it's time to leave your current job.

SUMMARY: Don't stay where you're tolerated, go where you're celebrated!

Value vs. Necessity

Sitting at the front of most 9-5 offices is usually a person who answers the phone and signs for packages. The term for this person has changed over the years from *Secretary*, to *Front Desk Person*, to *Administrative Assistant*, and I suspect it will continue to change. However, you know who I'm talking about. It's that person at the front.

Do you need that person? I sure think you do.

Oftentimes this person has been with the company for decades. They know where every piece of stationary is, where all the equipment is stored, who worked on what, who is doing what, and they are there all day every day to direct phone calls and receive packages. Plus, they seem to keep the kitchen/breakroom in tiptop shape and always have the coffee maker full.

They are an absolute necessity in most offices and the whole place falls apart when they are off on vacation or sick. In fact, they are so important that they either cannot ever take a vacation, or when they do we have to hire a temporary replacement for them. We can't go a single day without them. Do you know any other position at work where we have to hire a replacement when they take even a single afternoon off? I can't.

And yet…they most likely get paid the least amount of money of anyone else in the office.

That's crazy, isn't it?

Now let's think about the highest paid executive. It most likely is the CEO.

In 2019, the average American worker made $58,000 and the average CEO made $15 MILLION! That's a ratio of 270:1. In 1965, the ratio was 20:1.

Regardless of you thinking this is an obscene number or not, you have to admit that this trend is all across the corporate landscape. It seems as if the less work you do, the more money that you make. Why is that?

It's because of something I call "Necessity vs. Value."

The front desk person is a necessity. Without them, the office falls apart. However, their replacement (the "temp" that gets sent over from a "temp agency") is usually trained up and replacing them in a few short minutes. The Temp is just as much a necessity as the original worker.

However, Senior Executives add "Value." Maybe they went to college with someone who is an investment banker on Wall Street and they can introduce our CFO to them and help secure some financing for the next big merger. That adds tremendous value to the company. That one personal connection may start in motion a chain of events that leads the company to merge with their biggest competitor, thus creating a virtual monopoly and leading to total domination of the market. Because of this, 20% more workforce is hired, raises and bonuses are huge this year, and we all get to move into a brand new fancy office tower. That's value.

That same executive can do LITERALLY NOTHING for the rest of the year. Sure, they call into meetings and they go to conferences and they create the look of being busy...but they don't add anything that is necessary. All they did was add one thing of value – and it's going to pay off for years to come.

Now, the best place to be in is where you add both necessity AND value. The necessity-only people are easily replaced. The value-only people are usually kinda hated by their peers. "What does that guy do all day?" is a common question asked behind their backs.

If you can occasionally add value, and almost all the time add necessity, you will have job security and many promotions/raises in your future.

SUMMARY: Learn the difference between jobs that fulfil necessity and jobs that add value. Try to craft your position into one that does both.

Burning the Midnight Oil

Sometimes you have to work long hours – there's just sometimes no getting away from it.

There was a railway line that I used to inspect in Canada's arctic. The point of the railway was to transport people and supplies from Winnipeg (the largest city in central Canada) all the way up to a small town called Churchill, Manitoba. Fun Fact: Churchill is the "Polar Bear Capital of the world." During the winter it can get down to -60° F. It is WAY up there in Canada.

As my coworkers and I would inspect the train bridges, we were in a modified Ford F350 that drives right along the train tracks. It uses the rubber drive wheels of the truck to accelerate and brake, and there are steel guide wheels that flip down to lock onto the train tracks to keep the truck perfectly balanced.

We drove along the train tracks and we could only get off the tracks at road crossings. In a city, this isn't a problem – there are crossings every block. However, in the middle of nowhere, sometimes a crossing is a 4-hour drive away. The train track was a single track, so if there was a train coming in the opposite direction we had to back up for 4-hours to get off the tracks to get out of their way. It was a royal pain in the ass.

What we did to mitigate this problem is that we reserved a block of time when we were the only people on the tracks and we inspected for long hours in order to get from the first crossing to the second crossing. This meant we had to work an 18-hour day.

It was a slog and we were doing it in the summertime when temperatures were around 90° F and the bugs were so thick that we wore bee-keepers suits to try and keep them away. It was a rough time, but that's our job and we "enjoyed" it ;)

One reason why we enjoyed it is because we know it will pass. We know we will do this one intense inspection and then it will be done.

Unfortunately, there are people you work with (or maybe it's you) that keep working long long days all the time with no end in sight.

I once worked with a drafter who would work 18-hour days every day.

Why did he do that? Because his boss would give him a bridge to draft and he wouldn't stop until the entire bridge was drafted.

You can't draft a bridge in a day. They take weeks and/or months. However, he couldn't get that concept through his head. He wanted to just work work work until it was done and he did this by working 18 hours a day, every day. He once said to me "I don't like to have anything unfinished on my plate. I work until it's done."

Do you know how he was rewarded for finishing the bridge drawings in record time? His boss gave him another bridge to draft.

The point I'm trying to make here is that yes, sometimes you HAVE to work long hours, but a lot of the time you will just have an un-ending to-do list and you shouldn't kill yourself working 18 hours all day every day. The work will keep piling up. Work the number of hours you can (most people stick to 9-5, Monday-to-Friday) and then take a break. Work can wait. Don't kill yourself. You'll actually probably end up being MORE productive if you take breaks and walk away from work on a regular basis.

SUMMARY: Stop working 18-hour days. No one is impressed and your only reward will be that your boss will give you more work. Work a solid 9-5, Monday-to-Friday, then take a break. You'll probably actually end up being MORE productive.

Section Three:

Communicating with Others

Angry Angry Hippos

Never ever ever write an email and hit the "Send" button while angry.

It's perfectly ok to write an email while mad, but you must sleep on it and cool down before you go back to it, proof read it, reword it, and maybe not even send it.

This same advice applies for text messages and even phonecalls. What are you doing communicating while mad? I'll tell you what you're doing – you're technically high on the same chemical in your brain that is released when you snort methamphetamines. Would you think it wise to start hot rolling your best batch of Scooby snacks and then try to win an argument? No? Well then why are you sending an email while mad? It's the exact same thing.

SUMMARY: Never send an email or text message while you are angry. Cool down and sleep on it. Maybe don't even send it at all or at least proof read it and reword it before you send it.

To CC Bcc

Fill in the "To", "CC", and "Bcc" on emails as the LAST thing you do before you hit the send button.

Sometimes the send button and the save/close button are right beside each other. Sometimes you accidentally hit the send button when you were mouseing over to the attachments button.

You are most likely not going to send something incriminating or embarrassing – afterall, you were planning on emailing these people anyways – but you might end up sending an email that suddenly stops right in the middle of the

SUMMARY: Fill in the "To", "CC", and "Bcc" fields as the last thing you do before you send an email to avoid accidentally hitting send with an email that isn't finished yet.

Sayonara

Have you ever got an email from "Bill"?

They are asking you to do something, and you don't know who Bill is and you already have a lot on your plate so you don't reply and you forget about it.

A couple days later your boss says to you: "Why haven't you got those numbers to our CFO?"

You don't know what he's talking about.

"Yeah...our CFO, William Blakely."

If "Bill" would have signed his name with his actual name, his title, his phone number, his office location – you know, like a real email signature – then we wouldn't be in this mess.

It does not take long to set up an automatic email signature for your laptop and also your smartphone. If you are unable to figure out how to do that, ask someone in the office. You need to sign emails with a proper signature.

The first email you send to someone needs to have everything in it – name, credentials, title, company, location, phone number, maybe even mailing address and company website. Follow up emails can just be name and title...but you need to have this as a minimum.

SUMMARY: Make sure you have full automatic email signatures set up on your phone and your laptop.

Subpoena

Do you work for a large company? What's the definition of large? It depends. If you have multiple offices in multiple countries, then let's assume you work for a "large" company.

Do you know what happens at large companies? They get sued.

This happens at small companies as well, but not as often. If you work for a big company, you can assume there are at least a few lawsuits going on right at this moment. We're not talking large class-action take down the company lawsuits...we're talking wrongful dismissal, failure to make payments, breach of contract, and other fairly small "annoying" lawsuits.

And what gets subpoenaed during a lawsuit? The records. And what are the records of a company? Its emails.

Every email you ever write goes through a central server and gets saved there. There's a really good possibility that no one is reading them, but if there's ever a lawsuit, people start reading them.

Did you send an inappropriate joke to a coworker? Did that coworker a few years later get transferred to a different division? Did that division then get acquired by a different company? Did that different company then get accused of insider trading? Boom! Your joke is going to be found out because there's a chain of events that leads back to that employee and everyone that ever had anything to do with the new company gets all of their emails read.

Company text messages aren't recorded in the same way (yet) but by the time you are reading this book maybe they will be. The same goes for phone calls and maybe one day even in-person meetings.

SUMMARY: *Always assume that everything you write and/or say will one day maybe end up in court or on the front cover of the Wall Street Journal. Are you proud of what you said? Could you at least defend it?*

LOUD NOISES

Will Ferrell stared in the 2004 comedy hit "Anchorman" in which he plays the character of Ron Burgundy, a sexist, egotistical, over-the-top TV personality with a penchant for theatrics. During one exchange in the newsroom when Ron and the boys are arguing that the newest addition to the team (a woman) should not be allowed to be a co-anchor with Ron, one of Ron's coworkers, Brick Tamland, exclaims: "LOUD NOISES!!!" to try and make his point.

His point is not made.

It's meant as a ridiculous point that someone would think simply yelling out "LOUD NOISES!!!" would somehow win their argument, and yet I've seen it in meetings, to some extent.

W. Edwards Deming once said *"Don't raise your voice and assume this will convince others of your point. Instead, improve your argument. Find data to back up your points, because without data you're just another person with an opinion."*

The next time you're in a meeting or in a discussion where your opinion is the opposite of others, resist the temptation to raise your voice, name call, or do any of the other schoolyard tactics to "win" an argument. Instead, provide data to back up your opinion.

SUMMARY: Remember that data wins arguments, not raised voices.

J

I went to school with a guy, let's call him "J."

He was very smart. He got the highest grades.

I remember one day a bunch of us were hanging out in the student lounge and someone went over to J. They said "Hey man, how's it going?" J's response was "No, I haven't figured out how to do question #4."

The response from the guy standing there was "Oh…ok" and he walked away.

Obviously, he didn't really care how J was doing. He wasn't coming over to hang out. He was only interested in the answer to question #4 on our homework assignment.

How many people do you have in your life that you only talk to when you need something? Maybe there's a coworker that you have nothing in common with but you know they know how to do X and you call on them when you need X. Maybe you have a relative that is good at Y. You never talk to them for any other reason, except when you need Y. Or maybe you have a "friend" who is always available when you need someone to do Z. When you have a need to do some Z-ing, you give them a call. Otherwise, you never talk to them.

Stop doing that.

SUMMARY: Don't just talk to certain people when you need to get something out of them. You're not being a friend – you're being a parasite.

Saving Face

Each day at work and at home can be a minefield for arguments.

We face simple decisions such as "What should we eat tonight" all the way up to "Which department should we shut down?"

Decisions both large and small will all have various opinions in the room. Many times the opinions are valid and need to be heard and discussed.

However, sometimes some people's ideas are utterly stupid and they should be ashamed of the ridiculous words that came out of their mouth.

How do you deal with people who have bad ideas? How do you deal with someone that has all the right intentions but their idea will never ever work in a million years?

I always suggest that you "give people an out" and allow them to save face. It's never a good idea to make people look stupid, especially in front of their peers and bosses.

Here's an example.

When I was a junior engineer I was invited to join my boss at a meeting where very senior members of government would be discussing the situation with the city's major bridges.

There was a large suspension bridge that was in perfectly good shape except it didn't have enough travel lanes so there was always a traffic jam on it. Then there was a smaller suspension bridge located downstream that had less traffic lanes and was falling apart.

Originally the proposal was to demolish the small crappy bridge and build a brand new one, and also to demolish the larger suspension bridge (even though it's in good condition) and build an even larger bridge.

The highest ranking elected official in the room asked my boss if we could simply take the large suspension bridge, lift it up via helicopter, and fly it down river to the location of the smaller bridge. After all, we said it was in good condition, and the number of lanes that it currently has is the proposed number of lanes for the downstream bridge.

Yes, helicopters can lift things. Yes, they are used in logging and construction. But when a helicopter lifts something it lifts a single tree or a single piece of steel. The strongest heavy-haul helicopter in the world can only lift a mere fraction of a percent of an even smaller fraction of a single piece of a bridge.

My boss calmly said to him "A single helicopter cannot lift an entire bridge" to which he replied almost instantly "Well then let's get more than one helicopter!"

Instead of making him look like an idiot, my boss calmly turned to me and asked me if I could run the numbers and see how many helicopters would be required to lift the suspension bridge.

Please remember, this is a bridge similar in size to the Golden Gate Bridge in San Francisco.

I went back to my office, and counted up the number of bridge members in a section of the bridge, then multiplied it up to estimate the total number of bridge members (I wasn't going to count every single member) then multiplied it by the average weight of steel for an average sized beam. Now I have a giant number. I then looked up how much a heavy haul helicopter can lift and divided the two numbers.

It turns out, you'd need more helicopters than exist, all linked up together, all lifting in perfect unison to lift the bridge.

In keeping with our philosophy of "giving someone an out" we presented our findings in a short memo, complete with a few sketches.

Ultimately, we put the blame on the industry for not having access to the number of helicopters required.

The senior ranking government official read the report, and I've got to assume that at some point through it realized the stupidity of his question (but maybe not) and responded to it with "Thank you for considering this matter. I agree with you that it is not a feasible solution."

No one had to look stupid, no one had to walk out of the room with their tail between their legs. It's often a very human reaction to shoot down people's dumb ideas. This only causes them to get their back up against the wall and make them want to fight. It makes people want to double-down on their bad ideas just to prove a point.

The best approach to an argument or a difference of opinion or a really really stupid idea is to hear it out, maybe even point out some parts of it that make total sense, then calmly lay out why you think there may be a solution that is different yet similar that we can all get on board with.

I'm never a fan of making someone look stupid in front of others. They have a lot on their mind and you wouldn't appreciate it if someone did the same thing to you.

SUMMARY: Give someone an out. Allow them to save face. Don't make people feel stupid in front of their peers.

The Idiot in the Room

Let's say you've got someone on your team that shouldn't be there. Maybe they are the new guy who is clueless as to how to do anything. It's not his fault – he just got hired and literally hasn't learned a thing yet, but the boss assigned him to your team. Maybe the useless person on the team is the boss. It's fairly common in Corporate America that people get promoted to become leaders in their field, only to have a horizontal move across the organization. Now they are the head of a department that they know nothing about. They make more money than anyone else at the meeting, but they can't contribute in a meaningful positive way at all.

This struggle exists outside of the boardroom as well. You may have young kids who want to help make dinner or a nephew who really wants to help you decorate the Christmas tree. You don't want to crush their spirit. You don't want to tell them to go away. You don't really want their help either.

It seems like we know how to handle this dilemma with kids, yet we forget that the exact same technique will work in the boardroom as well.

When someone is incompetent and feels insecure because they are unable to contribute, ask them simple questions or give them simple tasks so they can feel like a big man.

I use the word "Man" because in my experience it is far more often that males in the workplace experience this.

Many men want to feel like they are dominating or at least in control of the situation. Many women feel this way as well. Certainly, both genders want to feel respected and feel like they are contributing.

It may be as simple as getting your nephew to hold one end of the lights while you put the rest up on the Christmas tree, or it may be asking a softball question to an executive that you know they will be able to answer or at least BS their way through.

SUMMARY: When someone is incompetent and feels insecure because they are unable to contribute, ask them simple questions or give them simple tasks so they can feel like a big man.

Feeling Smart

Everyone has a boss. Your boss has a boss. Your boss's boss has a boss. Even the CEO reports to someone – the shareholders and The Board. At the end of the day, everyone has someone that they report to and someone that they are trying to impress.

I have found that over my career, one of the best ways to get promotions and rise up the corporate ladder is to make my boss look good to their boss. This also works when I try to make my client look good to their boss as well.

Clients want to save money. They want a high quality product and they want it delivered on time. When you can do all three things, and especially if you can get them a deal and deliver earlier than expected, they look good to their boss. This philosophy works outside of Corporate America selling services to governments or other corporations – if you are selling a product to a consumer and you get it to them for a cheaper price and at a faster speed than they were imagining, they are able to say to their friends "Check out the great price I got on this and it was here right after I ordered it!" Now they are looking good to their friend group, and that is just as important as looking good to their boss.

SUMMARY: Make others feel smart and look good to their boss.

Proper Email Technique

How many emails do you send each day? Or how many text messages? Or how often do you make phone calls?

Chances are good that you communicate on a regular basis with multiple people.

How often do they reply to your messages and how often do you get the response that you wanted?

Do you ever ask a series of questions throughout an email and in the response the person only answers two of your five questions?

I used to struggle with written communication until I took *Professional Writing* at a local technical college.

I've used two methods ever since then and it has worked wonders for my ability to get the responses that I wanted.

There are two types of emails. The first one is when you want to get something out of someone, for example, you are asking a question about when they are going to finish the project. The second type is when you need to tell someone bad news, for example, you won't be getting them the deliverable on time and you've also blown the budget.

Through the techniques I learned, I've managed to increase the percentage of responses to my questions, and also decrease the amount of angry emails I get when I'm telling people bad news.

Approach #1: Asking Questions

The basic format of every email that intends on asking a question goes like this:

1) This is my question
2) Here is some background information that may help you in answering it
3) I'm ending the email by re-asking the question to you

That's it.

I have found my success rate in getting emails answered massively improves when this format is used.

At the risk of boring you with a poorly worded email, I'm going to show you an example of the exact same email written two different ways.

Let's start with a normal-sounding email that is NOT written in the proper style:

"Hello Marry-Anne,

How are things? I hope everything is going well with your dog – I remember you told me he was feeling a bit sick the last time we talked.

I'm over at headquarters right now and we are just running some of last quarter's numbers. Rick is here. Remember he said he was going to transfer from the Michigan office? Well, that got postponed and now he's still in Charlotte. We ran some numbers and weren't sure if we are supposed to close out this month's budget or not. Any ideas? There's a lot of talk going around the office about how things are going to be affected at next month's budget meeting. Are you going to be calling in?

I hope your dog is feeling better and you have yourself a happy and healthy weekend.

Good bye!

Cheryl"

From reading that email, you can hear the tone in Cheryl's voice. She is concerned about Marry-Anne's dog, she gives some news about Rick, and she had some budget questions and also wanted to know if Marry-Anne was calling into some meeting, or going to a meeting? I can't remember. There was too much going on in that email.

Now let's rewrite that exact same email, using the correct approach:

"Hello Marry-Anne,

Are we supposed to close out this month's budget or do we wait until next month?

I'm here with Rick in headquarters and we are discussing how close-out will affect next month's budget. We aren't sure if this gets recorded right now, or if it postpones until next month, so we wanted to check with you first before we close it.

Please let me know when the right time is to perform close-out on this month's budget.

Thanks,
Cheryl"

Notice how we removed all the fluff? To some people that might sound cold. You know what does sound cold? Constantly saying "Hi, how are you?" every single time you call someone and never even waiting to hear the response. If you actually care about Marry-Anne's dog, then send an email that is just about the dog – don't use it as some sort of excuse for trying to make it seem like you care about the dog when you really just care about the budget close-out.

Do we need to know that Rick hasn't transferred yet? Probably not. If we do, send that in a different email.

Is it relevant or important if Marry-Anne is going to call into next month's meeting? If it is, send an email or IM or text that goes like this: "Are you calling into next month's meeting?"

Every email you send needs to have one theme and one goal. The goal of this email is to find out if we are supposed to close the budget this month. That needs to be the first sentence, and it needs to also be the last sentence. You need to "control the action" so that as they are finishing reading the email (the short email) they know exactly how they are supposed to respond. Marry-Anne could respond to this email with one sentence: "Any time before the last Friday of the month at 11:59pm is the proper time to close the budget." With the original rambling email, she might not even get to the end of the email.

To reiterate how to write an email when asking a question:
1) This is my question
2) Here is some background information that may help you in answering it
3) I'm ending the email by re-asking the question to you

Approach #2: Telling bad news

The basic format of every email that intends on telling someone bad news goes like this:

1) Here's our understanding of what you wanted to have happen
2) Here's all the things that we got accomplished
3) Here's what happened to stop us from achieving our goal
4) Here's what we are going to do to make things right

Again, let's start with the wrong way to write a bad news email:

"Hello Marry-Anne,

I am so sorry, but we won't be getting those budget numbers done on time. Rick has been really busy with planning for the move and I forgot to remind him about him needing to fill out the form to get it into the system before end-of-day. I guess this probably screws a lot of things up for you, right?

Again, I'm so sorry.

Take Care!

Happy Friday!

Cheryl"

Now, let's rewrite this email using the proper approach:

"Hello Marry-Anne,

I understand that getting the budget numbers to you is an important step for project close out. Rick and I have worked diligently to make sure all the invoices have been either paid or marked as 30-day overpaid so that they are being accurately recorded in the system. Of the 16 invoices, all but 2 have been paid and we have reached out to the two remaining sub-consultants who have both told us that the payment should arrive by the end of the week. Furthermore, we balanced the Estimate-to-Complete column with the Actuals-to-Date so we won't be showing any errors during our financial review teleconference tomorrow.

Unfortunately, we have not been able to finish the final budget numbers just yet. Rick and I will work into the evening to get these numbers uploaded into the system and we should have everything in place by tomorrow's 10:00am meeting.

Cheryl"

This email is longer. It lays out all the good things that did get accomplished. It shows that Cheryl and Rick weren't goofing around – they've been working all day at this and it appears as if they simply ran out of time. Not only does it show all that got accomplished, it also gives a plan for how Cheryl and Rick are going to work this evening to make things right before tomorrow's meeting.

It's a bad news email, so it doesn't have the "have a great day" or "I love your dog" casualness that would come off as glib or not taking things seriously.

To reiterate how to write an email when you have to tell someone bad news:

1) Here's our understanding of what you wanted to have happen
2) Here's all the things that we got accomplished
3) Here's what happened to stop us from achieving our goal
4) Here's what we are going to do to make things right

SUMMARY:

The basic format of every email that intends on asking a question goes like this:

1) *This is my question*
2) *Here is some background information that may help you in answering it*
3) *I'm ending the email by re-asking the question to you*

The basic format of every email that intends on telling someone bad news goes like this:

1) *Here's our understanding of what you wanted to have happen*
2) *Here's all the things that we got accomplished*
3) *Here's what happened to stop us from achieving our goal*
4) *Here's what we are going to do to make things right*

Email Etiquette Part 4

I would say that at least once a year I get an email that was supposed to be a reply and ended up being a reply-all.

Our HR Department sent out an email reminding people that if they have any unusual health issues that aren't covered by our standard medical plan that they write back, let HR know the details, and then a specific plan could be tailored to their situation.

Someone hit the "Reply-All" button and now the entire company knows about his particularly embarrassing problem with his bowels.

A year later, a congratulations email was sent to a senior member of our team who had hit their 30-year anniversary. Someone hit the Reply-All button and went on a long diatribe about why they didn't get congratulated. Our sector manager continued the gag and replied all to let him know that his 30 years happens next month and they did not in fact forget him.

Reply and Reply-All are very different buttons in email. If you don't yet know what the difference is, please ask a coworker to describe it to you and make you realize why you must be very careful when hitting one instead of the other.

SUMMARY: Learn the difference between Reply and Reply-All buttons in email.

Ghost Phone Calls

Do you ever struggle with people around you not taking you seriously or not listening to what you say? Have you ever had some really bad news that you needed to tell someone but you were afraid that they wouldn't listen to you?

Well then using a "Ghost Phone Call" is the trick for you.

When I started in the industry, I was a site inspector. Between the ages of 19 and 23 I would routinely go to site where it was my job to tell men who were 19 to 23 years older than me what they were doing wrong, and that they had to rip it all out and start all over again because they didn't read the engineering plans properly.

This is not a technical problem. This is an external psychological problem.

How do I, an awkward engineer-in-training, who probably looks younger (and might actually be) than their kid, tell these large men what to do?

Enter: The Ghost Phone Call.

Now for starters, when I showed up to a jobsite I always made sure to introduce myself and ask for the foreman/superintendent or whoever is in charge. I politely let them know my name and that I'm here from the engineering company. I'm just here "to take a look around at some things and I might have some questions for you." It's also always good to make a little bit of small talk. My go-to question was always "You watch the game last night?" If they respond with "Yes" and if I didn't watch the game, then I say: "Oh man, I missed it, what happened?" If they respond with "No" I say: "Oh man, it was amazing!" Any follow up question can be resolved by saying "I didn't watch the end" and if they say something along the lines of "Wow, did you see that hit that Samuelson had?" I could just respond by repeating the exact same line back to them: "Oh man! What a hit by Samuelson!"

Whatever your technique is, don't just show up to the jobsite unannounced, and start walking around taking photos of people. No one likes that.

Now that I've introduced myself and asked if there's any safety orientation I need to go through, it's a fantastic idea to point out all the things that they are doing right. My job on site is to point out problems, so I'm the downer of the group. Instead of just saying negative things, I say things like "This safety fence you put up is looking good." Whatever I can say that is somewhat positive is a whole lot better than "This is wrong, this is also wrong, and this thing over here is very very wrong."

When/if I ever do find an issue, I make sure it is actually an issue. Many times contractors can find creative ways to install things that do not necessarily go the way the engineer designed them to. However, that does not mean that it won't work that way.

I needed to make sure that the thing that I was about to point out was wrong before I point it out because if it turns into a "Let's call your boss" moment and I am the one who ends up being wrong, this damages my credibility as a site inspector.

I find something wrong and I double check that it is in fact wrong. Do I call over the foreman and say "Hey Mike, I found something wrong"? Absolutely not.

The first words out of my mouth are "Hey Mike, can I ask you a question?"

Saying to someone "Can I ask you a question?" instantly raises their sense of self-worth. I look to them as being smarter than me and want them to impart their knowledge back to me. It's a very simple way of setting up a situation where someone is put at ease.

My first question is literally a question and one that I know they can answer:

"I want to make sure I'm looking at the right specification for the steel. Is this the one you are using?"

99% of the time Mike will say "Yes" but the 1% of the time he points out that I'm using an old specification saves me from embarrassing myself. If I'm looking at an old spec, of course it's going to be different than the new one.

Let's assume he responds by telling me that I am in fact looking at the most current version of the spec.

Now I say "And are we using Grade 300 steel here?"

At this point, he probably looks down at the steel and sees that it's clearly got a "Grade 200" stamp on it.

Without even answering my question, Mike will usually say something like "Oh…um…we just had that 200 steel sitting there but we were going to swap it out with 300 before we poured the concrete."

I know this is BS, but I got to give Mike a way of saving face. I found his error and he's correcting it. I never had to say "You're wrong" – he told me what he was going to do to fix it without me even having to ask him.

However, in rare cases the Mikes of the world will say "Nah, we don't want to use 300. I've used 200 before and it's all good."

This is where Ghost Phone Calls come in.

Mike isn't listening to me. He sees me as a kid. Even now that I am approaching the end of my inspection career and have seen it all, I still run into Mikes who don't want to listen to me, so I have to break out the occasional Ghost Phone Call.

I pick up the phone. I call a number. It doesn't matter what I type in, as long as I don't actually call anyone.

From 10 feet away (or whatever distance is required for Mike to be able to eavesdrop) I say "Hey boss, I'm just wondering if we really need to use the Grade 300 steel or not? Oh yeah? You sure? Cuz Mike's already put Grade 200 in. Has to be 300? For sure? It's gonna be a pain for him to take it out. Alright. I'll tell him."

(I would suggest practicing this script before you use it and make sure you bone up on your acting skills).

Mike will hear you. He heard you say "Hey boss" so whomever I'm talking to has authority. In the worst case scenario you can actually call the boss…but if you perfect the Ghost Phone Call well enough, you won't even have to. The authority is coming from whomever is on the phone, and you even tried to argue in Mike's favor. You don't look like the jerk – the "boss" on the phone is the jerk. Worst case scenario you actually do have to call the boss and he tells Mike to rip out the Grade 200 steel and use the 300.

SUMMARY: Politely introduce yourself, make small talk, and use Ghost Phone Calls when people don't take you seriously. Worst case scenario, use actual phone calls to the boss.

Keep it Simple

Your stories are probably too long, and your explanations are probably too detailed.

SUMMARY: Don't use ten words when nine words will work.

Disagreeing

We are all going to have to work with people that we disagree with. Meetings can sometimes get heated and emotions can rise.

Is this ok? Are we allowed to disagree and be passionate about our opinions? Of course we are.

I've worked on teams where the team leader says that everyone's opinion is valid and needs to be discussed. This is bullshit. Sometimes people have bad ideas. Sometimes what someone is saying is unsafe, illegal, unethical, or just plain stupid.

However, there are ways to shoot down someone's ideas without embarrassing them.

I am an opinionated person, but I still always try to err on the side of caution and hear people out. If the opinion that they are saying is simply wrong and nothing positive can be gleamed from it, it's time to disagree with them, politely, and move on.

GE's famous CEO Jack Welch was a huge fan on "candor" that is, the quality of being open and honest in expression, or "frankness", or "bluntness." Just say what you are thinking about someone's ideas, keep it short and professional, but to-the-point.

We need to have an office environment that allows for people to be frank with one another in a professional manner. If everyone is afraid to say anything negative at all, we run in circles and we will never get anything done.

Be frank, be direct, and do it in a polite and professional manner.

SUMMARY: Disagree with people, but do it in a professional, polite, and respectful manner. Stop beating around the bush. If you disagree with someone, keep it short and don't sugar coat it. People will appreciate your honesty.

Come Together

We each have a different upbringing, different schooling, and a different way of coming at the exact same problem. These differences and diversities of opinions can be a strength, but they can also lead to heated arguments.

How do we avoid getting each other's feelings hurt when we are discussing a problem?

A Prime Minister of Canada, Justin Trudeau, wrote a book called "Common Ground" in which he argued that we have far more similarities than differences, and that by seeing things from other people's perspective was the best way to negotiate.

There are other strategies for negotiating. Sometimes some people suggest starting with ridiculous demands and hope that at least one idea gets allowed. Getting up from the table and throwing a fit as you storm out of the room is also a common negotiation technique taught by others.

I personally think those types of negotiations are unprofessional and childish.

Regardless of your political stance being more liberal or conservative, I would hope that you see the value in Trudeau's way of thinking. We have ways in which we want to accomplish a goal, and we can get there in different ways, but the important thing is to try to find the common ground while we are deciding our path.

SUMMARY: When negotiating, try to see things from other people's perspectives and work towards a common goal.

Quiet Time

Monday to Friday, nine to five. These are the recognized hours for anyone that works an office job. Yet many of us show up to work quite a bit earlier than 9:00 am and a lot of us work well into the evenings.

We have smartphones and laptops and VPNs that allow us to work from home. Evenings and weekends are times when some of us claim we get our best work done.

Great. If that works for you, that's awesome.

But do you know what you shouldn't do outside the hours of nine to five, or outside of Monday to Friday? Email. Or call. Anyone that you work with ever.

Unless the building is on fire, or there's some other catastrophe that requires immediate action, you should never ever email or call anyone on the weekends or in the evenings.

Write an email and go up to the top under "Options" and click on "Delay Delivery." If you can't figure out how to do this, Google "How to delay the sending of an email in _____" and enter the name of your email program in the underlined section.

Never send an email before 9:00 am and never send one after 5:00 pm (if you are asking someone to do something for you).

If someone wanted those numbers ASAP, then use your discretion as to whether or not it's appropriate to send an email outside of normal business hours.

Go ahead and work whatever hours you want to, but let people have their quiet times when it's outside of normal business hours.

SUMMARY: Only send emails and make phone calls between the hours of 9:00 am and 5:00 pm, Monday to Friday. If you want to be an even better person, only email/call between 10:00 am and 4:00 pm and never call during lunch hour.

Use Your Words

Have you ever written an email or sent a text message and it was completely misunderstood and taken the exact opposite way that you intended it to be taken?

Written language can be tricky. Even if you have all the best intentions, it's difficult to convey tone of voice, sarcasm, passion, dismissiveness, anger, or happiness, by just using the type written form of communication.

I can't tell you the number of times that I've been a part of an interchange or heard from a coworker, friend, or family member how type written words were misinterpreted.

So do yourself a favor – pick up the phone and call them instead.

Calling allows for a quick back and forth. It clears the air.

I've had people call me, joking around, having a great time, and we are completely on the same page. Then, they end the conversation by saying "Alright buddy, I'll just shoot you a quick email that summarizes all this just so we have it written down. See ya!"

Then I get an email that is stiff, impolite, and comes off as rude.

If I never would have had the phone call with that guy, I would have thought he was a jerk. But now that I've talked with him, I see that his style of writing is stiff, whereas in real life he's a great guy.

Do yourself a favor and call people. Yes, follow it up with an email so there's a record of it, but always start with a phone call to save you a lot of headaches.

SUMMARY: Call people on the phone. Emails can come off as stiff, demanding, and rude. Call people first, then follow up with an email that summarizes what you called about.

Communication Breakdown

Have you ever given someone what you thought was and what you fully intended to be a compliment, yet they took it completely the wrong way and now they are mad at you?

Flip that coin around and ask yourself: Have I ever been the one who flipped out when someone was trying to compliment me?

Stop doing that.

People at work are going to write emails like "Even though this was delivered late, the client was still happy – thanks!"

Don't focus on the first part of that sentence. They went out of their way to try to thank you and they gave you a piece of good news that the client was happy.

You can go through life with a stick up your ass, or you can let things slide and reply to that email with: "Thanks! I enjoyed working on that project!"

Different people communicate differently. A lot of times they thought they were being nice, when you perceived it as being rude. Turn your thinking around. You must decide for yourself if you're going to let things bother you.

SUMMARY: When someone compliments you, take it as a compliment. Don't dissect exactly how they said it and try to find ways to get mad about it. Let it go. They thanked you, they complimented you. Take the win and move on.

Shitting

An "idiom" is a group of words that we all seem to understand what it means, but when it's translated literally it makes pretty much no sense at all.

English has a lot of these and it makes it supremely frustrating for people to learn our language. If this book ever gets published in another language, I want to thank you for reading it and sometimes struggling through it, because English (and probably the form I write in) is not the easiest to understand for those who have English as a second language.

The idiom I want to discuss in this chapter is: "Know your shit, and know when you are shit."

Know your shit:

This expression means "You need to be certain of what you are talking about."

If you are an expert and you know exactly how to solve the problem, now is the time for you to speak up and fix it for the rest of us. We are counting on you.

Know when you are shit:

This expression means "You need to have a self-awareness of when you are a complete idiot and you should not say anything when this is the case."

How many times have you been in a meeting and someone starts talking out of their ass and has literally no idea what they are talking about? They are just filling the air with their hot air. They are trying to convince the room that they are smart, but they are succeeding in doing the exact opposite.

Take a look in the mirror and ask yourself if you have ever fallen into this category. If you don't know what you are talking about, then it's time for you to sit there and not say a thing.

SUMMARY: Know your shit, and know when you are shit.

Let it Go

Disney's hit movie, *Frozen*, had worldwide sales of $1.3 billion on a $150 million budget, giving the studio almost a 9X return on their investment; this of course does not take into account all the extra money made on merchandizing. The hit song of the movie was *"Let it Go"* and was sung by the title character Elsa. If you were around children, tweens, teenagers, and even some adults during 2014 you could not escape hearing people sing it. *"Let it go"* cemented its place in common English as a reference to this movie.

I never watched *Frozen* and this chapter has nothing to do with it.

Do you have a boss or a relative that tells the same story over and over again? I once had a boss who had a run-in with a colleague. It turns out that the boss was right and the colleague was wrong, but the boss would keep bringing it up over and over again to the same people who were at the last meeting. We got it. Let it go.

Have you ever met someone who has a catch-phrase? Or maybe there's certain verbal ticks they use over and over again? I had a professor who would constantly say "Get the point?" That was his version of "Do ya know what I mean?" He said it so many times, we actually started tallying them up during class. His other saying was "Am right?" as in "Do you think that was the right way to solve this equation?" At the end of class we would see who won – the "Am right" team or the "Get the point" team. Prizes were awarded. Stats were kept on the season. A trophy was given out at the end of the semester.

This professor should have let his sayings go.

SUMMARY: Evaluate your stories, phrases, and everything that comes out of your mouth. Do you repeat them often? It's time to get some new stories. It's time to let the old ones go.

Singing in the Shower

Have you ever met someone who is really good at telling stories? Or maybe they have clever jokes that are actually funny and not uncomfortable groaners? Or maybe the way they present a verbal argument makes everyone else in the room stop dead in their tracks and agree with them?

Do you think they are freestyling these verbal displays? In all likelihood, they are probably not. They have probably practiced them either in front of others or when they are alone.

How much alone time do you get in a day? Maybe your commute to work is an alone time. Maybe you have the luxury of a large enough living quarters that you can get away to a garage or den or rooftop patio to have some time alone to think.

Even if you don't have any of these things, you most certainly shower alone, and the shower is where I bet a lot of the smooth-talking people in your life rehearse their lines.

Don't kid yourself and think that everything is made up on the spot. Some people have practiced that story/joke/argument over and over again.

You should start doing this as well.

Tell your stories to yourself the next time you are alone. Practice what you want to say in the next meeting. See if you can say the entire thing without saying "um", "uh", or other verbal ticks.

Good speakers don't freestyle – they practice; and the shower is as good a place as any to get in a few lines of practice.

SUMMARY: Use your alone time to practice phrases, sentences, and even entire stories/arguments in your head multiple times before you debut them in public.

Winning and Losing

Some people always have to win. It doesn't matter if it's a silly boardgame, their fantasy football league, the promotion at work, or the argument with their significant other. Some people have to win at all costs.

You know what happens to them? They generally end up losing.

Winning at all costs can cost you friends and family. It can cost you your health, both mentally and physically. It can cost you your life.

You've been in meetings where there's that guy that has to win the argument. Don't be like him.

You've been in relationships where the other person always has to be right. Don't be like them, and also get out of that relationship.

If someone says "The movie starts at 9:00 pm so we have lots of time" and you know it starts at 8:00 pm, that is a good and reasonable time to point out the error. You don't have to be a jerk about it, but it is a reasonable thing to be right about.

However, if someone says "I think the Braves are going to lose today" you don't have to be the person to point out how there's no way the Braves are going to lose today. Sometimes, let other people win the argument, or don't even start the argument. It's totally ok to agree with someone, even if they are wrong. If there's no negative consequences, then consider agreeing with them – there are other things in life worth stressing about.

SUMMARY: You don't have to win every argument. Don't be that guy. Sometimes (or a lot of the times) let other people win.

Reaching Out

We've never in history been more connected to one another, yet we still ignore people and let relationships fall apart. Who have you not talked to in a while that you should?

The problem with communication years ago is that a phone call could seem a bit too much, and since it was, people would avoid communication all together.

You have no excuse anymore because you could do something as simple as liking an Instagram post, or leaving a small comment. You could send a text, and you could build up to an email. Ultimately, you can make that phone call or physically visit that friend/relative that you've fallen out of touch with.

I'm writing this during a worldwide lockdown due to a virus pandemic. We have been forced to slow down and spend a LOT of time in our apartments/houses. It's given all of us a chance to get back to calling and connecting with our network of people. When we get out of this crisis, we need to not forget to connect.

Pick up the phone, send the email. Connect with others.

SUMMARY: Connect with people who you've maybe fallen out of touch with. Bury the hatchet if there was some bad blood there. Let's come together as a world.

Sunshine & Rainbows

Did you have anything to do with the latest terrorist attack? Did you sell the gun to the latest mass shooter? Are you a Greek God that controls the weather and you were the one who is causing the storm that is supposed to hit this weekend?

I'm going to assume that the answer to these questions are all "No."

Conversely, did you invent the latest drug treatment that is going to save all those lives? Are you that famous person who just donated a hundred million dollars to charity? Or did you just negotiate better health benefits for the entire company?

Again, I'm going to guess you had nothing to do with those things as well.

Both sets of events are news. Both sets of events are things that people in the office are going to be talking about.

Ask yourself: Which sets do I want to be associated with?

Yes, you had NOTHING to do with that terrorist attack. But do you need to be the one who brings it up? Also, you had NOTHING to do with everyone getting better dental coverage, but wouldn't it put a smile on people's faces when they hear the good news?

Just because something is news, does not mean you have to be the one who tells the whole office.

Bad news is going to get talked about. People are going to find out. Did Harold and Chelsey in accounting just tell everyone they are getting divorced? That's their news, not your news. You don't have to be the person who tells everyone else. I've seen it time and again where bad news is happening and people can't wait to share it with everyone else. Do you want that to be you? If it's bad, keep it to yourself. If it's good, share it. Create a reputation for yourself that you are the person bringing good news to others.

SUMMARY: Be the person that shares good news with everyone. Let someone else be the person that tells the office about the bad news.

Section Four:

How to be Ultra Productive

Pain then Pleasure

We've all stared down at a huge to-do list and wondered where to start. It sometimes seems impossible to even take a bite out of it.

I had a boss that taught me the "Pain then Pleasure" technique of tackling a to-do list. It goes something like this:

Your list is going to have things that you HATE doing, but you know you must do them. Maybe that's something like "Do your taxes."

Your list is going to have things that you really actually kinda want to do, like "Take a nap" or "Call your best friend."

My former boss suggested putting the tasks into two categories: Those that are painful and those that are pleasurable.

Now, take a step back, and run head-on into that task you HATE. I mean, you really hate it. It's going to be terrible. Do the most painful thing. It's on your list and you know you must do it. So…DO IT!

Then, one you've got it out of the way, reward yourself and do the easiest thing. Do the most pleasurable thing.

Did that feel good? That's nice. Now you are going to run your head into the wall and do the next most painful thing.

This alternating between pain and pleasure is a good way to smash that to-do list. Give it a try :)

SUMMARY: On your to-do list, alternate from doing the things you hate the most, with the things you really actually want to do. Pain, then pleasure. Repeat.

You've Got Mail

A never-ending flow of emails comes into your inbox every day.

That notification badge on your smartphone keeps increasing. We live in a world of over-communication with alerts and beeps and pings and dings that never seem to stop.

I had a colleague that had over 3,500 unread emails in his inbox. The IT Department warned him that if he didn't clean up his inbox, he would stop getting new emails.

What ultimately became the solution?

They opened up a second email address for him because management deemed his old emails too important to delete and too cumbersome to go through and organize.

First, let's start with spam emails. We all get them from time to time, but some of us get one a week, and some of us get twenty (or more) a day.

It takes roughly three months of dedicated spam-fighting to get your numbers down to one a week. You have to be diligent and fight it every day, but if you follow this simple advice I'm about to give you, you as well can be a certified spam-fighter and stop the endless flow of nonsense into your inbox.

It's really quite simple…you just NEED to do it every single time you get a spam email.

At the bottom of almost every single piece of advertising email, there exists in tiny little font the word "Unsubscribe." Trust me, it's in almost every piece of spam email. When you click on that link, it may open in a new browser and you may have to answer a multiple choice question for why you no longer want to receive these emails, but once you do this, it sets off a chain reaction that will massively help reduce the spam that you get.

There are only a few mass email servers in the world. Corporations from all over pay these companies to search for keywords in previous advertisement emails and then they pay for the access to people's email addresses to then get their advertisements sent to the same people.

That is why yesterday you got three separate emails related to product X and today you got two more that were also related to product X. They all are coming from the same email mailer server.

When you click "Unsubscribe" on one email, it updates in the system that this person is not interested in X. Companies pay a small fraction of a penny for each email that gets sent out on their behalf, but still all those thousands and millions of emails start to add up. They will have it in their contract that they do not want to pay to send emails to someone who has chosen to opt-out of an email related to their product.

This starts a chain reaction where all companies that sell X no longer will send you emails about their product and/or service.

But what about those other emails? What about the emails that are pertaining to Y?

Well, you just have to unsubscribe to them as well.

Each time you unsubscribe to one email you are removing ten other emails from coming in.

Conversely, each time you do not unsubscribe (within a 24 hour period) it tells the mailer that you may be interested and it signs you up for more emails.

You have to keep on top of it and unsubscribe every single time you see a new spam email.

If you do this, within three months you should have your spam emails down to practically zero.

The second types of highly annoying emails are from co-workers who keep sending you messages.

We all seem to have smartphones and if we don't we generally all have access to our emails quite easily. That is why, as soon as I get an email, I respond one of three ways: 1) Here is the answer; 2) I don't know the answer, but I think you should ask this person instead; or 3) Can I get that answer back to you by this time?

When someone sends you an email and you have the ability to answer it in five seconds, you should do it. Get it off your plate.

When someone asks you a question that you do not know the answer to, it's still quite helpful to them when you point them in the right direction.

Finally, when someone asks you to carry out a complex task or reply to a large email with a lot of opinions, it's also very helpful to them that you give them a timeframe for when you will get back to them.

Leaving that email just sitting as unread in your inbox does not help anyone.

SUMMARY: Respond to messages instantly. Either unsubscribe, answer the question, point them to someone else, or give them an estimate on when you'll be able to answer the email in detail.

Keep Chipping Away

If you're like me, you have a lot of "Big Projects" on the go. You've got books you are reading (or writing), you've got that home renovation, the car you're working on, your crafts, your garden, that musical instrument you're trying to learn, the round-the-world trip you're planning, and of course you've got all those projects at work that are enormous.

If we look back at all the things we are trying to do, it's a wonder how we get anything accomplished.

One trick that I've found that works well for me, is to take on projects that don't go in reverse when they get neglected.

For example, a garden goes in reverse when it is neglected. If you fail to water your plants, they die.

Another example project that goes in reverse is learning a new language or a new musical instrument. If you stop working on it for a long time, you forget what you learned…and the project dies.

For that reason, I like to take on projects that don't die when they are neglected. That way, I can keep chipping away at them for days, weeks, months, or even years. Eventually they get finished and I have something to show for my efforts. Writing a book certainly falls into this category. Building something. Renovating something. Creating a piece of art or doing a craft. These all fall into this category.

I'm not suggesting that we never invest time into projects that have the possibility of going backwards. Your own personal health is a good example. If you stop exercising and stop eating healthy, it is very bad for you. But just because your own personal health is a project that can go backwards, does not mean you should avoid working on it.

What I'm saying is, don't take on too many projects that can go backwards when they are neglected.

SUMMARY: Try to choose projects that don't go in reverse when they are neglected for a period of time. Keep chipping away at them, and eventually you'll finish.

Biting & Chewing

You've heard the expression "Don't bite off more than you can chew" but you've maybe also heard the expression "Bite off more than you can chew." Which one are you supposed to follow?

I'm a big advocate for doing the first one for as long as you can, and then switching it up.

With "Don't bite off more than you can chew" you have time to relax. You can focus on the things that really matter to you. By saying no to people, by not starting that new project, and by taking more time to relax and unwind, you give yourself time to reset. Hit that snooze button on life and slow things down a bit. You don't have to always be go go go.

However, if you've been hitting the snooze button for too long, it may be time to ramp things up. There are a lot of things out there that you can add to your list and maybe it's time to bite off way more than you can chew.

Starting a business is a huge step. Proposing to your significant other, starting a family, joining a new sports team or transitioning to a whole new company – there are some big steps that can dramatically change your life. They may have huge upside potential, and they may crash and burn – you won't know until you try.

If you've been coasting for a while, maybe it's time to bite off more than you can chew and dive head first into that giant project.

SUMMARY: At points in your life you need to make sure you aren't biting off more than you can chew. Slow things down, take a breath, and take time for yourself. However, if you've been coasting for a long time, it may be that you need to start biting off more than you can chew. Flip between these two states throughout your life – don't stay in one forever.

Homebody Part 1

You probably work in an office. You probably wake up earlier than you want to, put on clothes, make yourself look presentable, get in your car or walk to the bus/train, commute to work, and make your way to your office or cubicle. Then, you might put on your noise-cancelling headphones and spend the rest of your day emailing, calling, and joining teleconferences. Then you commute home.

Why did you need to go to an office to do that? Why couldn't you have done that from home?

Many jobs need to be done in person. If you work a physical job, that needs to be done in person. If you sell things, face-to-face interaction is a million times better than selling things on the phone.

Sure, there are millions of jobs that have to be done in person…but there are millions of jobs that certainly can be done remotely, whether that is your home, a hotel, or a beach – it really shouldn't matter.

As I write this, my wife and I are under government-mandated quarantine, only allowed to leave our home to get groceries. This is because a worldwide disease called COVID-19 is infecting people all across the world.

However, I am, my team is, and her entire team are all able to continue to do our work from home. I start my mornings by checking emails, checking in with the team, looking at our budgets and schedules, then creating a report as to where we are falling behind and where we are getting ahead. I'm working as a *Project Management Analyst* for a multi-billion dollar infrastructure improvement project that is set for construction in two years in downtown Chicago. Our team members are located all across North America – and this "work from home" order hasn't slowed down design one bit. In fact, I've seen an increase in productivity across the team.

So why do people commute to an office? After this virus pandemic is over, will there be a massive influx of people going back to the office tower? I sure hope not.

We used to be largely an agricultural society. Everyone was self-sufficient and worked their own land. Then we shifted to an industrial manufacturing society. With the invention of large-scale transport cargo ships and international flights, manufacturing has shifted overseas. Our society here in North America has shifted to a services-based economy. Take a look at the back of your iPhone or Apple laptop – it will say *"Designed in America, Manufactured in China."*

There's nothing wrong with compartmentalizing our industries by region. You relax in your living room, you cook in your kitchen, eat in your dining room, sleep in your bedroom, and work on your car in the garage. If you started working on your car in the kitchen it would be somewhat possible, but still a stupid idea.

Compartmentalizing the world is also not a bad idea. We are manufacturing products overseas and we are designing them here. There is a risk of globalization hurting us – supply chains being disrupted during international crisis, trade wars, currency manipulation – but these arguments are outside of the purview of this book. I want to make an argument for working from home.

I've been working from home for years. I can easily work across time zones, states, provinces, and countries. If I've got a call at 8:00 am Eastern Time and I happen to be on the West Coast, it's not a huge deal. I can wake up at 4:45 am, take the call from my bed and literally go back to sleep right after the call. Try doing that from an office. You can't.

With smartphones, great internet, Skype, Zoom, GoToMeeting, MS Teams, webcams, and all the other technologies that connect us, I seriously scratch my head and wonder why we still have 95% of our staff coming into an office.

Young employees do need face-to-face guidance. They will still need to have people right there holding their hands. I am not advocating for 100% work-from-home, but certainly a massive reduction in Monday-Friday office work can be accomplished in the service/consulting industry. It will just take initiative from Upper Management.

SUMMARY: Ask your boss if you can work from home.

Homebody Part 2

How do you stay productive after you've convinced your boss to let you work from home?

There are two things to focus on: Internal and External.

Internal is how you stay productive and External is how you show your boss that you are still getting things done.

Internal:

I wake up at the same time every day. I need to stay in that routine. Turning off your alarm and sleeping until you naturally wake up is a terrible idea. Are you not getting enough sleep? Then be an adult and go to bed earlier. You have cut out the commute time of your job, so that extra 30 to 60 minutes can do wonders for you. I try every day to be completely ready to go at 9:00 am every day.

Some people still get dressed in their business clothes. This works for some, and this seems like overkill for others. Do what works best for you. If you have a lot of webcam calls, then yes, you do need to dress appropriately.

Keep taking your lunch hour. Instead of sitting in the breakroom eating reheated leftovers and listening to Mike talk about his golf game, you can sit out on your porch, go into your backyard, spend some time on your couch, or go hang out in the amenity area of your building. But still, keep it to the regular lunch hour.

A proper home set-up is key. Many of us have the luxury of a room in our home that is our office. Get two monitors, a comfy office chair, close the door to distractions, and actually get work done. If you don't have this space luxury, invest in good noise-cancelling headphones, sit at the kitchen table and get some work done. I would recommend against sitting in bed or on the couch. That posture for 8 hours a day will kill your back. Get serious. Get professional. Sit at a table and do some real work.

Finally, know when to turn it off. You worked 9-5 at the office, so work 9-5 at home. When that clock hits 5, you are done. Log out. Turn off. Good job.

External:

I've found that during this current COVID-19 pandemic that my team has been more connected and sent more emails. It's important that we keep doing our regular meetings. Nothing is different. We've got team members spread all across America and Canada and we keep each other apprised of what we are doing.

This worldwide virus has caused a lot of sickness, death, loss of income, and sadness for many people, but we can find a silver lining. It is forcing us to work from home, and when this is all over, many of us will hopefully keep working from home. It's better for our mental health, it (so far) has seemed to actually increase productivity, and with less people commuting it's better for our air quality.

SUMMARY: When working from home, internally make sure you are in a good professional routine and treat this seriously. Externally, make sure you are keeping in regular touch with the team.

Why do we Win?

Why do some people "make it to the top" and others flounder? Why do some people seem to get all the breaks and others seem to constantly strike out? Is there a magic formula for success? Is there a way to predict who will win and who will lose?

I've read many self-help books and discussed this subject with many friends, family members, and coworkers over the years. We've discussed how Jim and Bob both have the same parents, went to the same school, did all the same sports, but Jim made it to the big leagues and Bob never got a single scholarship to play ball.

Why does Sue always seem to get those big promotions at work when John is just as smart but is stuck in the same position? Is there any pattern that we can see?

Luck plays a big part in success. We've all heard the phrase "being at the right place at the right time."

Hard work plays a big role as well. If you're sitting next to a hiring manager on a plane you are in the right place at the right time…but if you haven't put in the hard work to have any of the skills that they are looking for they aren't going to hire you.

So is luck-plus-hard-work the ticket? Is that as simple as it gets?

I've found that there is a third element of success that goes beyond luck plus hard work and that is: "Willingness to act." You have to actually make that jump.

Let's look at a few scenarios:

In the dating world a lot is initially built on looks. Let's say you are in your mid-twenties and you are looking to date. You are at a party and you see someone who has the look you find attractive. You are in the right place at the right time. You can check the "luck" box.

Hopefully, they are also single and looking to date. This is another check in the "luck" column.

You look a certain way and hopefully that is also a look they are into. This is partly "luck" but this is also partly "hard work." Regardless of how you look, it takes effort to look the way you do. You've worked hard on your hair/clothes/body and hopefully they like what they see.

But luck and hard work won't get you a date with that person across the room. You need to walk over there and talk to them. You have to have "Willingness to act."

At work, you work hard to know the technical ins and outs of your field of practice. Susan just announced that she is retiring. You have the hard work under your belt and you just had the stroke of luck you needed – Susan is retiring and they need someone to replace her.

But you also need the third element: You need to be willing to act.

You need to go talk to your boss and let them know that you are wanting to take over Susan's position. You need to take that step. Hard work and luck alone won't get you there.

I once had the opportunity to move to a new country to get a big promotion. I had done the hard work, luck had shined upon me as there was a potential opening...but I had to take that GIANT leap of moving to a whole new country. I had to have willingness to act.

We spend a lot of time "working hard" and then get depressed when life doesn't turn out well for us. We need to play the game and try multiple things to increase our chances of getting lucky. It's pretty hard to play one round of roulette and win a lot of money. But it's also pretty hard to play a hundred rounds and never win. Luckily for us, there are a lot of chances in life that we can take that don't cost us money, whereas playing roulette endlessly will lose us our house.

Consider talking to your boss about getting that promotion, or asking what steps you should start to take to be in line for a promotion in a few years. You're going to have to have some luck during that conversation, but it won't cost you anything if the conversation doesn't go the way you want it to.

And of course, when the boss says "We really need someone to take on this job, but you'll have to be willing to do _____" then you have to be willing to act.

Luck gets you far. Hard work gets you far. But you need that final step: Willingness to act.

SUMMARY: Success comes from the combination of three things: Luck, Hard work, and Willingness to Act. Luck comes and goes, hard work we seem to be willing to put the time into, but we must also be willing to act when an opportunity comes along.

Albert Einstein

$E=MC^2$ is what Einstein is known for. Despite this being an insanely popular equation, I really doubt any of us could actually explain it, other than just reciting what each variable stands for. How this applies to everyday life, and how this somehow creates an atomic bomb is pretty darn confusing for most of us.

Einstein said a lot of things throughout his life but one sentence that has stuck with me is "Make things as simple as possible but not simpler."

I've strived throughout my career to clean up and simplify and it has paid off huge dividends.

We can start with physical things. Is your desk a mess? Your filing cabinet full of old useless things? It can be a monumental task to clean it all in one day but you don't have to. You can set aside the last 10 minutes of each day to do some form of cleaning. Throw out that old stack of papers that you don't need anymore. Get rid of those cables that are useless. But what happens if you need one of those cables one day? Then buy a new one.

Go through your files and archive things you don't need on a regular basis. External storage hard drives are getting cheaper and cheaper. You can fit everything you've ever done onto one of them and by the time it's full, I'm sure Western Digital has developed one that has double the storage capacity.

Check out your resume. Does it still have your job at Taco Bell on there? If you just graduated from college and this is your first job, then keeping your Taco Bell job on there makes sense. It's tough working in the fast food industry. You need to deal with a bunch of customers who are jerks and you work long hours. But eventually you need to take your summer jobs off the resume. Clean up and simplify.

Is that safety document getting larger and larger? There may be ways to consolidate information into easier to read bite sized chunks. Clean up and simplify. Do your emails go on and on and ramble? Do you put too much info into your correspondence? Clean up and simplify.

SUMMARY: Clean up and simplify your life.

Record Keeping

Many people are born into their parents' house and don't move out until they go off to college. Maybe you had a family that moved around a lot because one parent was in the military or had another job that had them relocating, but it's pretty likely this wasn't the case and you lived in one home from birth until college.

Throughout college you maybe lived in dorms. After college you probably bounced around from crappy apartment to dumpy house with roommates. Eventually (hopefully) you settle down and get a decent apartment or maybe even take out a mortgage on a house.

If you're keeping track, by the age of 30 you might have lived in six places. Maybe your number is significantly higher, but it probably isn't much lower.

Do you know the street address including the zip code of each of those places and the month/year you moved in and out?

If you didn't write it down as it was happening, it's going to be pretty difficult to figure it out. You'll have to look through a lot of photos, message a bunch of friends, try to find email receipts for things you bought etc. to try and figure out your exact history.

Why would you ever need to know this? Well, I needed to know this when I was applying for a TSA Precheck FastPass through the airport. If you are ever applying for citizenship of a different country or applying to a high-security level government job you will also need to know this.

I know what you're thinking: But I don't travel enough to need FastPass, I will never pursue citizenship of another country, and top secret government jobs aren't for me.

However, this was just one example.

There are a lot of things that we do in our life that years from now we may need to know.

Where is your birth certificate stored? What was your log-in information to your college transcripts website? What was the phone number or email of that previous employer that you could one day get a good reference from?

Keeping track of things is now easier than ever. You have a computer. You have Google Drive. You have access to infinite ways to back up important information. Yet many of us don't do it.

How many important contacts do you have on your phone, yet some of us haven't linked it to Google Contacts and if we ever drop our phone and it breaks we lose hundreds if not thousands of contacts. Back up your phone. What about all the photos you have? Are they stored on an external hard drive or saved to iCloud? Because if they aren't you might lose them.

The number of passwords we must memorize is getting ridiculous. Number, upper case, lower case, symbol, can't be similar to previous passwords, has to be changed every 6 months – how can we remember all this? If we don't have a central place where things are written down we will forget. We have life events that are important that we tell ourselves we will remember, but the truth is if we don't write them down then we won't.

Back things up. Save things (online or on a hard drive). Make lists. Keep your resume up to date with references and the dates when you took those online courses. Keep track of your mailing addresses.

It takes minutes to add things to your "Master List" wherever it is that you keep it. Come up with whatever system you want to come up with. Keep a system in place so when you do need to know that thing it will be an easy few clicks to figure it out, instead of hours of painful password resets and asking old friends if they remember that thing you need to know in order to apply for that new job or fill out that form for the government.

My dad used to keep track of every new pair of shoes I got. That's taking things too far, but chances are you are on the other side of the spectrum. It probably wouldn't hurt if you started to keep track of a FEW more things, right?

SUMMARY: Back things up. Save constantly. Record important things. Make lists of stats and track records. Update your resume and keep on top of things.

Billionaires

When Bill Gates, Warren Buffet, Jeff Bezos, Mark Zuckerberg, or any of the other world's billionaires enter a room, everyone hangs on their every word.

Bill Gates can do a TED talk on literally any subject and it will be the most listened to TED talk that month.

Sure, these guys are all very smart and very successful. But does that mean that they never make mistakes ever?

Leaders are surrounded by followers. They are also surrounded by advisors. An "Advisor" can be a fantastic job. You probably get to go to the fancy meetings with world leaders, ride in the motorcade or on the private jet. You rub elbows with other advisors and other heads of industry. It's a tricky line to walk though, because you don't want to tell your boss that they are an idiot and that this newest brain-child idea is actually quite dumb. That sort of "advice" could get you fired.

Because of this, advisors start to slip into the category of "followers" instead of advisors. They spend a lot of their time not necessarily advising, but moreso trying to come up with more and more creative ways to tell their boss that his hair-brained idea is a good one.

And therein lies the rub – the advice the boss is getting is turning into crap because advisors just want to keep their job.

I write this section to people who are in the boss/manager position. You are going to have advisors. If you are the head of a country (first of all, very cool that you are reading my book – thank you) you are going to have paid advisors that regularly go on TV to defend you. If you are a CEO or President of a company you will probably have a position designated for your advisor or team of advisors.

But managers at a much lower level have advisors as well. They might not have the fancy title, but they are advisors – and they might not be giving you great advice.

Take the new intern. They are wanting to make a good impression. Maybe you only have 5 more years of experience on them, but they report to you, so essentially you are their boss.

Do you think they are going to tell you that your idea sucks? I think not.

And this is the problem. We oftentimes (or all the times) go to people who report to us to get feedback on our ideas. Of course they are going to be biased and give us false positive feedback. We are the ones who are either expressly in charge of their promotion/raise or we at least have a lot more say in influencing it than they do.

If you want real advice, you need to go to people who make more money than you, are higher up the corporate food chain, or have absolutely nothing to do with you and either work in a totally different division or maybe even at a different company. Going to people who report to you for advice about your new idea is a pretty dumb idea. You can try it, but don't be surprised when everyone thinks your idea is great.

SUMMARY: No one tells billionaires that their idea is stupid. Rarely does someone tell their boss how dumb his idea is. If you want real feedback on your idea, ask people who make more money than you, are higher up the corporate food chain, or are completely disconnected from you. Then you can get some actual feedback.

Running

Whether you have a physical struggle to go exercise or a mental struggle to get up off the couch and write that email or make that phone call, we all face problems with motivation.

Where does motivation come from? This is a topic Tony Robbins tries to tackle in his hit books *Unlimited Power* and *Awaken the Giant Within*.

I'd recommend those two books of his. There's a lot of timeless wisdom and motivational pieces throughout them.

Motivation can be contagious. Robbins in-person talks are electric. He runs out onto the stage to pump-up music complete with a light/smoke show. The whole crowd is jumping and dancing. It's pretty much impossible not to feel pumped up if you're there in person.

Most of us will not attend an event in person. Or spend time watching a NetFlix special about him. Or even read his books. Most of us will sit on a couch and not do a thing.

That's sad, but that's the way the world is. Some people are motivated and some people are not. Some people are motivated for a short amount of time and then the energy dies. There's no magic bullet to motivation. If there was, self-help gurus and motivational speakers would all go out of business because someone had solved it and we all would start doing that person's technique.

How often have we told ourselves that we are going to go for a run, but then it's kinda cloudy out so we don't do it? Or we say we are going to call our great-aunt and wish her a happy birthday, but then we see that our battery is running low on our phone so we put it off to tomorrow? (and then we never do it.)

It's easy to go for a run when it's sunny outside. It's easy to cross other things off our to-do list when the timing and conditions are perfect. But guess what? It's not always sunny and conditions are rarely ever perfect.

If we keep waiting for the perfect time to do that thing that we want to do, we will never do the thing. There are a huge number of things that get in our way. There's no magic bullet to getting things done – we just need to do it.

SUMMARY: It's easy to go for a run when it's sunny out – but it's not always sunny. You need to find motivation to cross things off your to-do list without waiting for the "perfect time" to do them...because the "perfect time" may never come.

Section Five:
How to Manage a Project

Coach vs. Captain

Have you ever had a Project Manager that gives out orders, but never seems to do any work themselves? Are you frustrated with bosses that tell you what to do, but they themselves seem incapable of doing what they expect of you?

In my experience there are two types of leaders: Coaches and Captains.

NOTE: I once gave this presentation to a room where there were a few people to whom English was their second language and they associated "Captains" with the people that command an ocean vessel. That is not the type I am meaning. I am meaning the term captain as in the person on a sports team who is (generally) the best player.

Coach:

Coaches are great. We all need them. We need people to cheer us on, give us advice, tell us when we are messing up, and generally be able to see the big picture.

But when you watch sports, what do you notice? The coach is on the sidelines. The coach is on the bench. The coach rarely leaves the dugout.

Unfortunately, we have an epidemic in Corporate America of people who act like coaches but are on the court all the time.

If you're a coach, be a coach…and stay on the sidelines.

The "Coach" style of leadership, in a Corporate America setting, should be at all the meetings and check in with the team. The coach needs to have a vision for the future, anecdotal stories about the past that are helpful for the current situation, and good connections across the company so that we can get the resources we need.

A coach should not be getting into the weeds of day-to-day operations.

Captain:

A Captain actively contributes.

On a sports team, the Captain is scoring goals, setting up their teammates, and is (generally) the best player on the team.

Likewise, in a corporate setting, you need to have someone on the team that gets shit done.

They know the ins and outs of the software, or they understand exactly how the machine works.

You have a problem? You can go to them for actual help. If you went to a Coach, you'd get a bunch of stories and a big waste of time.

Both coaches and captains are needed. Sometimes the same person can fulfill the same role, but they have to realize when the team needs a coach and when the team needs a captain.

There's nothing worse than a coach on the court, and a captain on the bench.

SUMMARY: Teams need Captains – active contributors that are experts in their field; and they also need Coaches – cheerleaders, motivators, and people who can take a step back and see the big picture. Figure out what your team needs and when your team needs it, and don't give them the opposite of what they need, which is a Coach who is on the court and a Captain who is on the bench.

Chains

At some point in your career, you are going to have younger employees reporting to you. Maybe this will happen early on, or maybe it will take a while, but at some point there will be greenhorns asking you how to do things.

Will it drive you up the wall at their uselessness? It might. Please remember that you were once in their shoes.

I can be an energetic guy at times, so throughout my career my superiors have thought I'd do well in training the new folks around the office. The truth is, regardless of my energy, I love working with young people. Their sense of optimism is contagious and I love telling them all the ways I've made mistakes over the years and how they can avoid the same screwups.

I've been with the same company since I graduated from college so I'm about as familiar with the internal processes as is possible.

Still, there are a lot of processes and it's a monumental task to teach someone everything.

Something that has worked well for me is to give new employees the end goal and see if they can figure out the steps to getting there.

I sure want to tell them exactly how to do it step-by-step. I want to hold their hand and walk them through the tried and true way of doing the thing I've told them to do.

However, when you take the chains off, when you let people fail, they learn the lesson far better than if you were to tell them, and in some cases they actually figure out a smarter, faster, better way of doing what you wanted them to do. This is how innovation is born – by letting people find their own path.

As long as you watch over them and make sure they aren't about to hurt themselves, the company's reputation, or do something that can't be undone, it will be a worthwhile exercise to let people fail.

SUMMARY: Tell people the end goal, then let them figure out their own path. Take the chains off. They may surprise you with a new innovation.

...but it comes heated up

We've all been in a hurry before. We're supposed to be at the meeting in an hour, we know it's going to take at least 45 minutes to train over and that walk plus elevator takes forever. We have got to get going and there's no time for lunch.

I was in this exact situation once and I wanted to grab a super quick bite to eat. I ran into a coffee shop, pointed at one of the pre-made sandwiches, and told the guy behind the counter: "I'll take that one right there, I'm in a bit of a rush, so you don't need to heat it up."

He looked at me and said "But sir, it comes heated up."

I replied "Yes, I know you usually heat it up but I'm in a big hurry so if you could just hand it to me I'll pay for it and be on my way."

"But sir...it comes heated up."

"Yes, I know that, but I'm about to miss my train so can you please just hand me the sandwich and I'll be on my way?"

"Umm...but...uh, it comes heated up."

At this point I realized arguing with this guy is getting me nowhere so I let him heat up my sandwich and I ran to the train just barely making it in time.

This story, at first, demonstrates one important point, but after repeating it to multiple people I eventually realized that it demonstrates a second important point I had not originally seen.

Point #1 – Not everything has to fit into the perfect set of rules

I did not want my sandwich heated up. You are going to have clients who want something that is slightly outside of what you normally do. Do you want to lose clients? Well, a good way to do that is to never bend the rules of what you normally do.

This same idea goes for within the corporation as well. How many times have you had an invoice that needs to look slightly different than the standard form and someone in accounting refuses to change it up? Or maybe you need to download a slightly different piece of software than the company usually uses, but the IT guy won't let you install it because it goes against company policy. It's not illegal, unsafe, or unethical – it's literally just a slightly different piece of software that is going to do the job far better than what we are currently using.

People who are sticklers for rules that make no sense slow down progress and stifle innovation.

If the customer doesn't want their sandwich heated up, don't heat it up.

Point #2 – There may be a good reason for that dumb rule

I've told this story many times. I still stick by the central point that rules can be worked outside of if we are keeping things safe, legal, and ethical.

However, after telling this story multiple times, someone who used to work at a coffee shop said to me: "It's a FoodSafe rule that certain types of sandwiches need to be heated up to kill off any potential bacteria. If he didn't heat up your sandwich and you got sick, you could have sued the coffee shop."

That stopped me dead in my tracks. He was absolutely right. I owe that sandwich guy an apology.

Or do I?

The second point that this story demonstrates is that sometimes that rule that seems dumb is actually absolutely necessary and if the reason for its necessity was explained then people would have a much better time following it.

How many times does the Foreman at the factory say to the new employee: "Don't touch that pipe."?

If he gives his warning and moves on, will the new employee care? Will they even remember?

Now how about this modification: "Don't touch that pipe because it isn't grounded properly and if you touch it, 5,000 volts of electricity will go through you and kill you instantly. We're gonna get it fixed up sometime next week, but until then, don't touch it. Probably safe to not touch it ever anyways."

Now is that warning going to be listened to? Of course it is.

Just telling someone a rule is sometimes not enough – people sometimes need to realize the reason behind the rule.

SUMMARY: Remember that not everything has to fit into the perfect set of preset rules. However, also remember that there may be a good reason for that seemingly dumb rule and make sure to seek it out before you break it.

Iterations

There are different types of sales jobs. Many of us think of slick advertising campaigns with social media marketing, TV ads, radio ads, billboards, and "traditional" marketing techniques.

There is, however, a huge world of sales that is spent responding to "RFPs".

If you don't know what an RFP is, this chapter is probably not for you. However, it's pretty short, so you might want to learn something new, no?

An RFP stands for "Request for Proposal" and it is the way that most governments hire companies to do work for them. Do all the windows in the capital building need cleaning? A Request for Proposal will be posted to a government bidding website. Does a brand-new bridge need to be built? You don't just look up "Bridge Builder" on Google – the government puts an RFP up on their website asking for qualified bridge builders to submit a proposal.

Now the process can get really complicated; it's the government – everything is slow and complicated. There are sometimes levels before the RFP such as the RFEI which stands for "Request for Expression of Interest." Companies don't give any price quotes or talk about how they will do the thing they are trying to do; all they do is write a letter expressing that they are interested in one day presenting a proposal.

There's "Requests for Qualifications" which is basically when bidding companies send in corporate resumes of who will be potentially working on the project.

There's a few more, but I won't bore you. The only thing you need to know is that there are generally a lot of steps to doing work when you want to work for the government.

I've been the Proposal Manager for hundreds of proposals over the years, and one trick that I use to get ahead of the competition is: Iterative Proposals.

This technique is highly frowned upon by a lot of people simply because "That's not the way things are done around here." I ask them: "Is there anything unsafe, illegal, or unethical about it?" There's a long pause. "Well…um…no. But that's just not the way we do things."

If they are my boss, then I have to listen to them. However, usually they aren't and I'm in charge of the proposal so I can go ahead and do this technique.

Most people are trained to make their proposals absolutely perfect before the client sees them. There are multiple revisions and multiple meetings were things are discussed over and over again. Is the client invited to these meetings? Never. Is the client kept in the loop on what we are developing for them? Never.

And what a stupid idea that is.

I've suggested that we involve the client right from the beginning. Let's say they've asked for a brand-new pedestrian bridge to be designed and built in the middle of a park. They are light on the details of what they want. The RFP simply says: "A bridge is to be designed and constructed that spans 50 feet and is located at these GPS coordinates."

From the very get-go, I try to get a meeting with the client. I want to figure out what their budget is and what type of bridge they want. I can start by proposing something: "How do you feel about a steel bridge that is made off-site and put together Lego-style when it gets there? It could cost about $100,000 for engineering and $500,000 more to fully install it. Does that sound good to you?"

You will learn a lot from their reaction. If the client says "Yeah, that's kinda what I was thinking" then you are off to the races. However, I've had clients say "Oh man, this is a remote park that hardly anyone uses. We were moreso kinda thinking you would just fall an old tree and hikers would walk across the fallen oak tree. Could we do the whole thing for under $5,000?"

Now, depending on the size of projects you normally work on this might be right up your alley, or might be far too small for you to bid on. You'll sure save yourself a lot of time if you would have asked these questions right up front and figured that out quick.

I once worked on a proposal and we quoted the client close to a million dollars for the engineering. The winning bid was 1/10th of our price. Obviously they were looking for something completely different from what we were proposing.

I've had it go the other way as well. I've been called up by the client and they say "Did you forget a zero in the price proposal? Every one of your competitors were at least 10X more expensive than you."

There's a chance we have a totally different technique and that is in fact what we should be charging for our services. There's also a possibility that we left a lot of money on the table.

The point I'm trying to make is that you need to involve your client in the process from an early stage. It is totally ok to send them a draft of your proposal. You need to make sure you are not giving too much away because they may tell the other teams, so sometimes a phone call is a better strategy.

If you don't work for government clients and let's say you do home renovations, this is also a good technique to use.

Start by asking what someone's budget is. You can craft your services around that.

We in marketing sometimes spend far too much time doing what we think the client wants and not actually checking in with the client. Henry Ford once said "If I had asked the general public what they wanted they would have said 'A faster horse'" and because of quotes like this us people in sales have been trained to think that the customer is stupid. Steve Jobs once said "I don't ask people what they want, I tell people what they want." Again, quotes like this further drive home the point that the customer is stupid and we need to educate them. At times, yes we do, but at times we also need to involve them. Finding that balance is the tricky part that we all need to work on.

SUMMARY: Involve your client early on when you are coming up with your proposal. Don't wait until your proposal is perfected to finally present it – you may be way out to lunch and nowhere even close to what they were thinking.

Real Progress

Have you ever worked with someone who is constantly spinning like a top? They have a million things on the go, are constantly in meetings, looked disheveled, are usually pretty annoyed/angry/stressed, and have a to-do list the length of a pharmacy store shopping receipt?

...and yet they still don't really seem to accomplish much of anything?

That is because they are confusing "Motion" with "Progress."

Never confuse motion with progress.

You can spend an awful lot of time throughout your day running around and make it look like you got something accomplished, but when you step back, you actually did nothing.

Take a personal inventory of all the things you do in a day. All the phone calls you make, all the emails you send, all the other things you fill your day with and ask yourself "Am I making any actual progress on the task that the boss gave me? Or am I just making it look like I'm doing things?"

SUMMARY: Don't confuse "Motion" with "Progress."

Young Drivers

Have you ever worked on a team where there's this one guy that really doesn't care that the project is going sideways? It might not even be his fault, but he doesn't seem to care at all that the ship is sinking, even though he's on the same ship as everyone else.

Before I was a Project Manger at a large engineering corporation, I worked as a building inspector. I remember one day, as a junior inspector, that I was on site with the senior inspector of this new construction project. It was a giant parking garage structure right in the middle of downtown. Hundreds of carpenters and other trades professionals were running around this site – it was a beehive of activity.

I was on site to inspect the steel reinforcing bars that were being installed, before the concrete was poured two days later.

I noticed that the team of "rodbusters" (as they are called in the business) were just starting to put in the first few bars. I noticed that they were putting them in upside down.

Now you have to understand that engineering drawings are not exactly the easiest things to read, and they could definitely be forgiven for putting the bars in an upside down orientation.

I pointed out this to my boss and was about to walk over to tell them their mistake when he said to me "Wait a minute. Today we are here to inspect the plywood formwork. The rebar steel inspection isn't supposed to happen for another two days."

So here we were, standing just a few feet away from a team of rodbusters, who are all putting in the bars upside down. I was the junior, so I couldn't really argue at this point with my boss. We left the site, came back two days later, and sure enough, the entire parking structure had to have its rebar ripped out and put back in the correct way.

This is an absolutely asinine way of "teaching someone a lesson." I agree that it wasn't specifically rebar inspection day – but we are all on the same ship, and it makes us all look good when the project goes well. Just because it wasn't your responsibility to point out the problem or do something about it, doesn't mean you aren't still involved in this colossal mistake.

I wasn't in charge of this rebar situation, and there was nothing I could do about it. However, I couldn't help but remember a lesson I learned when I was sixteen years old that directly applied to this situation; it was a lesson I learned while taking a Young Drivers training course.

It was a hot Saturday afternoon, and there I was, crammed into a room with twenty other rambunctious teenagers. The instructor enters the room. He says we are going to start with a simple pop-quiz. The room moans, and at the same time is worried because none of us have even started to read the drivers manual, let alone are we ready for a pop quiz.

"First question", he states, "You are stopped at a stop light. Someone rear-ends you. Is it your fault, or is it the other person's fault?"

I think to myself "Yes! An easy one to start. It's obviously the other person's fault."

He continues: "You park your car. You go inside to go shopping. You come back out and someone has pulled their car out and scratched the entire side of your car. Is it your fault, or is it the other person's fault?"

Of course, I think I know the answer to this one as well. It's obviously the other person's fault. Right?

He asks his final question: "It's two o'clock in the morning. You are driving home from a party. You're sober. You have a green light. You drive through the green light and a drunk driver T-Bones you. Is it your fault, or is it the other person's fault?"

At this point I start to think I should ask for my money back. All these questions are all so obvious. I have done nothing wrong in any of these hypothetical situations. It's always the other person's fault.

The instructor asks the class "How many people think in each one of these situations it was always the other person's fault?"

Everyone puts up their hands.

He pauses.

Then he yells at the entire class "YOU'RE ALL WRONG!"

He goes on to explain that yes, from a legal point of view, the rear-ender is at fault, the person who can't pull out of a parking spot is at fault, and the intoxicated T-Bone driver is at fault. But then he says "But YOU are still the person who has a sore neck from being rear-ended, a scratched-up car, and you're also dead because you got T-boned."

Just because you are at a stop light, that does not mean that you can check out and take a nap. You are still actively sitting in traffic. There are people walking and biking and driving all around you. Think of a more ridiculous situation where you are parked at a red light and a semi-truck has lost its brakes. Its flying down the hill, surging towards you, blaring its horn and trying to warn you to get out of the way. Think of how big of an idiot (and also possibly a dead person) you would be if you simply sat there in your vehicle stubbornly saying to yourself "It's HIS fault if he hits me. I'm going to just sit here because it's my legal right to sit still at this stop light."

You're right. You're also dead.

The situation of parking – it is the other driver's responsibility to NOT hit you when they are pulling out of their spot. However, if you would have parked not so close to them, or if you would have parked five spots over in a spot that had no one on either side, you wouldn't have to be going to a body shop right now.

And finally, it's two o'clock in the morning. What percentage of people on the road are drunk driving? I don't know the exact number, but I can tell you that it's higher than zero percent.

Yes, you have every legal right to drive through that green light…but giving a quick left-right head turn as you are approaching an intersection can save you from getting dead.

At the end of the day, just because it's the legal thing you are entitled to do, or just because it wasn't your exact action item to address whatever the problem is, don't be that guy that sees the problem and does nothing about it.

To summarize this idea, I'm reminded of a time that I worked in construction with a French-Canadian guy named Manuel. He had an expression (that probably sounds better in French) that sums up this idea of how you should care when the ship is sinking, even if you aren't the captain: "Make everything your onion."

I'm not sure why it's an onion, but the point remains: We are all in this together so don't sit there cross-armed, not caring about the failing project.

SUMMARY: "Make everything your onion." Just because you might not technically be in charge of it, remember that you're on the same ship as the rest of the team.

Task Master

Don't you just hate it when you have a boss who tells everyone what to do, then becomes an absentee landlord who you won't see for days/weeks, only to pop back in to meetings and demand why things aren't done the way they wanted them to be?

I've had bosses who had extremely vague directions, only to have exacting expectations that the project be carried out in an extremely particular fashion.

Don't be like those people.

In Tony Robbins book *Unlimited Power*, he talks about these types of bosses who may think that they are leading, but really they are delegating tasks and responsibilities to others, only to be annoyed when things don't get done the way they want them to be done.

He rails against delegating saying that being a task master is not a valid form of leadership – it's just laziness.

Instead of being a task master, Robbins advocates for a different form of assigning jobs to team members and a different way of looking at things. His word for this is "leveraging."

Let's say I have a complex set of accounting tasks that need to be completed. We've got staff charging to various different codes to record their time, but many of them have been charging to the wrong numbers. Therefore, the budgets of some line items are being completely blown apart, while other line items haven't even been touched.

Moving the time to the proper line items is a job for an accountant or someone else in administration that has the proper permissions in the internal software accounting system.

What many bosses would do is to delegate this task to someone, let's call him Robby. Robby is told "We need to move hours around to a place where they make sense." That's his entire directive. Now Robby opens up a massive spreadsheet, only to see dozens of employees (who he probably does not know) and hundreds/thousands of hours charged to line items that at best may have a vague two-word description such as "Data Collection" and at worst may just have a number such as 34500.

How on earth can Robby know who has done what and where hours need to be moved?

The answer: He can't.

We are in this bad spot because Robby's boss has delegated this task to him. He is way in over his head and there's no way he'll be able to do it properly.

But Robby does not want to get laid off, so he spends the next four days moving time from one line item to another line item, in a balancing fashion so that it looks like each job has roughly the same amount of time being spent on it. Oh, and since the fifth day is a Friday and no one wants to ask for more work at the end of the week, he pretends the task took him five days.

Where does Robby charge his time? He splits it over a few random lines of this same project, thus creating more confusion and chipping away more at an already over-stretched budget.

However, there is another approach his boss could have taken to avoid this fiasco – that technique is called "leveraging."

Robby clearly needs to be involved in fixing this problem. He is the only person with software permissions to be able to move people's time around. The alternative would be to ask each individual person to go into their previous ten weeks' worth of time sheets and move time around.

That would be like herding cats.

We definitely need someone, like Robby, with access to the internal accounting system. But instead of leaving Robby to the wolves for him to figure this out himself, a good boss who uses leverage would sit down with Robby. The act of saying "Move his hours there and move her hours here" takes two seconds. The mouse-clicks and "next" "next" "approve" that will have to be done on the computer can possibly take ten to twenty seconds per movement.

It's a pointless waste of time for a boss to sit there while Robby does each correction, but it's incredibly useful for them to print out a list of all the team members, all the time charges, and then use a red pen to mark things up.

The boss (hopefully) knows everyone on the team, and if they don't, they need to invite the minimum number of managers to a meeting so that they can blast through each person's time charges.

Once it's all marked up, Robby is off to the races and he can spend just a few hours moving the time around.

This is leveraging. The boss needs to be there to make the decisions about where the time needs to be moved, the managers need to be there to explain who so-and-so is and what they have been working on, and Robby needs to be there to actually execute the orders to move the time.

Everyone at the meeting has a purpose and everyone is contributing.

This is leveraging. We used people's abilities and strengths and don't just throw them a giant project that they have no way of possibly completing on their own, only to have them fake it in order to not get laid off.

SUMMARY: Don't delegate – Leverage instead.

Move On

Do you ever spend time in meetings where everyone keeps arguing in circles about the best way to do something? You've got your way of doing it, and so do three other people at the meeting. Is your way the best? Well, you think it's a pretty good way of doing it and we've done it this way a few times before. What about Karl's way? It sounds pretty reasonable, but it's definitely different from your way. And of course there's Ken. He always has a different way to doing things. He's not wrong…but you just don't want to do it that way.

So what do you do?

I used to have this dilemma all the time. When working in an engineering office, there are always differences of opinion. You might think that math is all black and white, but there are many ways to come to a solution of a problem. There are small arguments (like what grade of steel would make the most amount of sense?) and then there are large arguments (like should we put in a bridge or a tunnel?).

One line that I come back to again and again is: "Hey folks…is what I'm proposing safe, legal, and ethical?"

There will always be differences of opinion. People will always want to do it their way. Ultimately, the job needs to get done and if you can't prove to me that it's unsafe, illegal, or unethical, then you really have no grounds to stand on for why we shouldn't do it my way, other than "Well, uh…I just want to do it a different way instead."

At the outset of the project, there will be a team leader or project manager chosen. It is his or her decision as to what direction the project goes. It's perfectly fine for dissenting opinions, but at some point you have got to make a decision as to what we are going to do.

You can argue endlessly in circles as to what is the better choice, but in a group of people with different backgrounds and different experiences, there will always be people arguing and you may never reach a consensus.

Projects are not democracies and they certainly do not need 100% agreement. They are (usually) dictatorships run by the Project Manager.

If you are the PM, you need to stay polite and professional, but you do get the final say.

Let the various team members make their arguments for why they want things to be done their way, then simply ask yourself "Is it safe, legal, and ethical?" And if it is, then you have every right to choose what the team is going to do and move on.

Don't worry, there will be multiple more decisions to make throughout the project and you will continue to have to make these decisions. You'll sometimes make the right ones and you'll sometimes make the wrong ones, but by keeping to the "Safe/Legal/Ethical" mantra you will be in good shape.

SUMMARY: At each decision point, ask yourself of the various options "Is it safe? Is it legal? Is it ethical? If it's a "yes" to all three, then you have every right to choose that option and move on. Keep the ship going forward.

Cleaning Crew

Do you have a mess that you need to clean up?

This question could be a literal mess (your child has just exploded the lasagna leftovers all over the kitchen floor) or it can be a figurative mess (the budget numbers are out to lunch and we're showing negative profit when we know it should be positive).

When I was a teenager, I volunteered at a summer camp on the cleaning crew. The team leader walked us through the process for cleaning the bathroom.

He posed the questions to us: "Where do we start? Does it matter? Do we start at the back of the room and work towards the door? Do we start at the door and work our way in? Do we randomly clean whatever we feel like? Is there a specific way, or does it not matter at all?"

Now, let me set the scene here. Our team leader was in his twenties and we were all teenagers. We barely knew how to (or wanted to) make our own bed. Most of us had little experience in doing laundry or cleaning much of anything.

We all shouted out various answers and I personally didn't think that there really was any one set way of cleaning something. Just clean all of it, right?

Wrong.

The simplest way to remember how to clean up a mess is put by this simple phrase:

"Cleanest to dirtiest, top to bottom."

Let's look at a real-life literal example.

The cleanest part of a bathroom is going to be the walls. Most people never touch walls in a bathroom, but there are still germs stuck to them. We start by wiping down the walls. We move onto the mirrors, as most people don't touch them either. The next items that we clean are all the handles, as these definitely get touched. We then clean the sink countertop, the sink, and ultimately move to the toilets. We rub down the top of the toilet, the back, the seat, the bowl, and then to finish the whole cleaning process off we mop the floors.

We have cleaned the bathroom cleanest to dirtiest, top to bottom.

The main reason we do this is to lessen the spread of germs because if we started with the floor and still need to move around the bathroom, we are sliding around, turning dust on our shoes into mud. Now the floor looks like a mess.

If we use a rag to clean the bowl and then use it to clean the toilet handle, we would literally be smearing feces on the handle. And good luck cleaning the sink THEN cleaning the mirror. You won't be able to see your own reflection in it because it will be so dirty.

Do you finish with cleaning the walls? With what? Your super-dirty rag? It'll look like you're painting them with a weak brown watercolor paint brush.

As you can see, it doesn't take much explaining to agree that "Cleanest to dirtiest, top to bottom" makes the most amount of sense when you are literally cleaning something...so why don't we take this same advice to heart when we are cleaning up a figurative mess?

All too often I see people brought into projects that are going sideways to clean them up, and they immediately start by tackling the biggest problem, while ignoring the very small (yet still present) other problems.

They think that by making big moves and decisive actions that all the other small issues will sort themselves out.

Well, this is exactly like taking a mop and flinging it all around a dirty bathroom – not only do you not clean up the big messes, but the small messes get covered in poop as well (figuratively).

When I have been brought on to help get problem projects back on track, I start by getting a full understanding of the project. Listening and learning is Step #1. It will be pretty apparent what is going wrong but instead of tackling those giant issues, start with the smaller things that are pretty close to being correct, but still need some tweaking.

Keep moving up to larger and larger issues.

What you will see by doing the "Cleanest to dirtiest, top to bottom" approach is that the larger problems start to fix themselves while you were focusing on fixing the smaller issues.

SUMMARY: When cleaning something up (whether literal or figuratively) start with the cleanest item that still needs just a bit more cleaning. Continue to clean from cleanest to dirtiest. Do not start by tackling the big issue or the dirtiest item. Cleanest to dirtiest, top to bottom.

Steve Jobs

When we're working on projects, there's the finished product that the client will see and then there's the backend work that will probably never get seen.

Generally, we will all agree that the final product needs to be aesthetically pleasing, slick, shiny, colorful, or whatever polished version we think the client will be impressed with.

But what about the things that the client will never see? Do we care about how that looks as well?

The creator of the Apple Computer Company, Steve Jobs, had a number of sayings and pieces of advice. If you want to spend hours entertaining yourself on YouTube, just search "Steve Jobs Advice" and you'll find countless videos where he pontificates about life and business.

One piece of advice that has stuck with me is when Steve said "Make a computer as beautiful on the inside as it is on the outside."

Have you ever compared a PC laptop with an Apple laptop?

Just flip one upside down and look at the underside. The Apple laptop will have almost zero screws visible or no visible vents, whereas most PC laptops look terrible on their undersides.

What about the inside of a desktop computer? If you've ever taken apart a PC, you'll see wires going every which way. But if you've ever taken apart an Apple desktop, you'll see that the insides are beautiful.

This goes beyond the hardware. Steve Jobs made sure this philosophy extended to the software and even the packaging.

As I write this, Apple is the largest computer company in the world and dominates its rivals such as HP, Dell, and Toshiba in terms of market cap. It was the "World's First Trillion Dollar Company."

Because of Apple's success, many other companies are starting to follow with slick marketing campaigns, better packaging, and yes, they are even starting to make the inside of their computers look as beautiful as the outside.

Take this approach and apply it to things outside of physical products.

If you work in a consulting business and your deliverable is a report, take pride in your rough notes. Organize those design binders or those project briefs. Just because a client will never see all the work you are doing on the back end does not mean you shouldn't try to keep it neat and organized.

Yes, Steve meant his advice to be taken literally because he wanted his products to be only put out to market when they are at their perfection, but you should also take his advice figuratively and make it apply to all the work that you do.

SUMMARY: Make sure the hidden parts of your product or service are just as beautiful and polished as the parts you intend for your client to see.

Schedule Budget Quality

As Project Managers, we tend to struggle with the questions "Where are we at with the budget?" and "Will it be done on time?" The quality of the product is often an afterthought.

I used to argue with perfectionists that shouted "It isn't perfect yet!" who do and redo deliverables over and over, only to improve the quality in areas few (or no-one) will ever notice, but who also succeeded in blowing the budget and delivering a week late. It would routinely become my job to explain to the client why we need more money and won't have it done in time "But don't worry", I would tell them, "…you'll love the quality."

That is why I've learned to sit down with my team at the very onset of the project to lay out my opinion of how we should approach schedule, budget, and quality.

Instead of entering into an argument, where everyone in the room will have their own differing opinion, I start by laying out the various options and what their shortcomings are.

Let's start with "Quality is #1."

What defines "Quality"? How perfect does the product need to be before we can send it to market? You can literally go in circles for infinity, trying to make the quality "perfect" and you will never achieve this intangible and unmeasurable goal.

Yes, there are minimum standards for safety. I'm not saying we need to strive for the minimum. What I'm saying is that we need to have some metric by which we measure quality by, and once we are at it, we need to stop running in circles endlessly trying to improve the quality – which is what we would have to do if we lived in a world where "Quality is #1."

Now let's examine "The budget is the most important thing."

How do we determine budgets? A lot of times, someone multiple corporate levels above us, who may or may not have anything to do with the project, and may also not know what they are talking about, dictates the budget. Each week the Project Manager checks the timesheets and the internal accounting systems (which never work well, are always a week delayed, and need a translator to understand) and see that we are "under budget." That's great. Of course we are going to be under budget (especially if the budget is a large dollar amount) because the job has just started.

But how do we know that if we keep doing what we're doing if we'll finish the budget but be nowhere even close to finishing the project or being ready to deliver the product to market?

This happens when we put budget as #1. Money is an unending charge code that people who are underutilized put their time to…but then one day, the money is gone and the project is halfway complete.

So this leads me to the conclusion that you are hopefully also coming to: Schedule is the most important aspect of a successful project delivery.

When schedule is #1, we can run through hypothetical situations and make actual calculatable projections.

We start out by breaking the project into the various stages. We assign the people who we think will be working on the tasks. We can all sit around a table and make reasonable guesses at how long it will take Bob to complete his task. It's sometimes a little bit awkward, but we do need to know how much Bob makes and whether or not we will be marking up his salary to cover the costs of overhead and profit margin (for confidentiality, this does not have to be done in a public setting and can be done in a small group of HR reps and managers).

Now that we have a tentative schedule with all the team members laid out including their hourly rates, we use Microsoft Excel and we instantly get a budget. The best part of this method is that throughout the schedule we put line items in for…wait for it…quality!

We can do a quality check every time we reach a major milestone. Whether this is a safety test of a physical product, or an aesthetical test of a design, or a calculation check of a complex set of calculations – we have it built into our schedule various checks and balances that make quality a top priority...albeit the 3rd priority.

By sitting down with the entire team at the outset of the project and asking everyone if they think the schedule is doable, it gets buy-in from each team member. If I ask you "Can you finish this aspect of the project in a week?" it is a tangible, measurable item and by breaking it down to days or at least a week or two, you can give me an honest answer.

Conversely, if I ask you "Can you complete this task for $10,000?" you may have no idea what that translates to in terms of hours of work.

And of course, the very stupid question "Can you make this perfect?" has no correct answer.

Therefore, sit down with your team at the beginning of the project, brainstorm the various tasks required to complete the project, get buy-in from each team member as to how much time they'll need (then add some time because people don't always estimate themselves properly), calculate the budget based on this input, and make sure there's stop points for quality checks.

SUMMARY: Start with a schedule, calculate a budget, and build in quality checks.

Section Six:

How to Improve Your Work Life

Whack-a-Mole

A lot of problems we face in Corporate America regarding being overworked are due to not staying on top of things.

You might get an email that asks a question and carbon-copies four other people. You might be the one who knows the answer, but the four other people might start chiming in. Pretty soon, you've got a chat room going on in your inbox. You have ten unread emails because people are all guessing at the answers, cc'ing everyone, when you are really the only one who should answer the question.

Or maybe there's an expense that needs approving. You get an email reminder about it. And then you get another email reminder the next day. You keep getting the same reminder over and over until you deal with it.

I try to visualize the carnival game "Whack-a-Mole" in order to help me cope with these types of situations.

In the game "Whack-a-mole" you have a giant hammer and there are a series of holes in a tabletop. The head of a mole pops out of the holes and it's your job to whack the mole back down into their hole.

If you whack it in time, you get points. If you do not whack it in time before it goes back into its hole, not only do you lose points, but next time two moles will come up. Now you must react twice as fast to hit both moles.

This analogy is the same as dealing with the tasks that are flying at you in Corporate America.

Each time a new email comes through, WHACK IT! Especially if it's an email where multiple people are carbon copied. If you don't whack it quickly, other people are going to hit "Reply-All" and you'll have a bigger mess to deal with.

When you have an expense to approve, approve it. The more you wait, the more emails you're going to get about it.

SUMMARY: As much as you can, treat each new task like the game "Whack-a-Mole." Whack those tasks so they don't start multiplying.

The Riddler

Have you ever had a boss that constantly makes the wrong decisions? Or a Team Lead that is so incompetent you wonder why they ever got hired, let alone promoted into their position of power?

I've been blessed to have many good bosses over my career. I've had fantastic mentors and learned more than any MBA could have taught me from some of my mentors.

Unfortunately, I've also been in your shoes and I know exactly what it is like to work for a complete idiot.

In the 90's, there used to be a show on television called "*Batman: The Animated Series.*" This show can be watched by (and I think was supposed to be watched by) children aged 9-12, but their older siblings, their older cousins, and their even older parents/uncles/aunts would also sit at the TV and watch it as well.

Without dating myself, I'll let you know I was somewhere between the ages of 9 and 50 when I watched *Batman: The Animated Series*, and a line from it has stuck with me my entire corporate career.

There's a scene where it shows the origin of one of Batman's arch-nemesis, a villain who goes by the name "The Riddler." He wears an all-green suit that is covered in question marks, and after he robs a bank or pulls off one of his many illegal activities, he always leaves behind a trail of clues for Batman to solve.

Why on earth a criminal would be so stupid to do this is beyond me. Just rob the bank and leave the scene, right?

Anyways, it is not for me to give The Riddler tips on how to pull of illegal activities.

During the scene where it shows the origin of the Riddler, his alter-ego, Edward Nigma, is shown at his desk job. He works for the Gotham Newspaper and is responsible for creating the crossword puzzles. Now in today's modern time with computers, it is all done via a complex algorithm, but back in the day those crossword puzzles were written by just a small group of very smart people.

Edward Nigma (The Riddler) is one of those "very smart people."

There's a scene where he is walking through the endless lines of cubicles, and he accidentally bumps into his jerk of a boss, causing his boss to drop his coffee cup. The boss yells out "Watch where you're going, you idiot!" to which Edward responds "I'll have you know sir, I am no idiot. Why, I would hazard a guess that I am actually the smartest person in this entire organization."

The line that his boss replies with has stuck with me for decades. He replies "Oh yeah? Well if you're so smart, then why aren't you rich?"

You could swap out "rich" with "Why aren't you the boss?" or "Why aren't you happy?" or "Why aren't you where you want to be?"

The reality is that there are many people who are "smart" but they hate their job, they hate their position, and yet they keep telling themselves how smart they are.

I have worked with many people who have Masters Degrees and Ph.Ds. However, despite their scholarly accolades, a lot of them are not happy. They show up to work at 7am, eat lunch at their cubicle, don't leave their cubicle until 7pm, and even come in on weekends. Meanwhile, the receptionist works 9-5, puts the phone on Do-Not-Disturb during her one-hour lunch break, and completely forgets about work in the evenings and on weekends.

Who is "smarter"?

Whether it's a lower corporate level admin person who doesn't stress about their job, or it's a high level Vice President who seems incompetent, the reality is that many times they are in a better spot than you are in.

The question is: What are you going to do about it to change it?

There are really three options.

The first option is to rise up. Get a promotion. Become their boss. I've done this before. Man, it really feels great to have someone reporting to you that you once reported to. But don't be a jerk about it. Don't be smug. Be as professional and kind as possible. Be the boss to them that you wish they were to you.

The second option is to move down. We've all heard stories of corporate executives who quit their jobs to go work at a grocery store or start a flower shop. One of my first bosses was the fourth largest shareholder at the company – he quit and became a food truck driver for a food bank.

Some may call it early retirement; some may call it a mid-life crisis. I call it "Finding what makes you happy." We don't all have to continuously strive to rise up the corporate ladder. Sometimes we need to cash out.

The third and final option is to just live with it. Sometimes we have bad bosses. Sometimes we have ridiculous forms to fill out at work that make absolutely no sense. We can choose to get annoyed at these things.

We can also choose to not let it bother us. I can hear the younger version of myself say "That's easy for you to say." And yes, it is easy for me to say. It's easy for you to say as well. There's lots of things in life that can frustrate us. We, however, are the ones who decide to get frustrated at them.

SUMMARY: If you're smart, make sure that you rise up, cash out, or adapt.

Figure it Out

Do you have employees who ask too many questions? They may think they are doing the right thing by letting you make decisions for them, but at the end of the day you can't get any work done because of the constant barrage of people waiting outside your office, wanting you to tell them what to do or how to do it.

Now flip the coin: Maybe you are the one standing outside the door or waiting for an email reply or a call back. If you are a junior employee it may seem like you spend most of your days asking senior employees questions and are constantly waiting for replies.

You may think this is the right thing to do, but let's be honest: From your boss's point of view, you are just another person asking more questions and filling their day with more distractions.

I used to have a boss that said the evenings and weekends are the only time they can do actual work because that's the only time people leave them alone.

Think of a job where you spend 9-5 Monday to Friday answering other people's questions and solving other people's mistakes and then you spend 5pm to 11pm Monday to Friday and all weekend long working on your own questions and mistakes.

This is why bosses are often so stressed out and why they work so many hours, and also why they get paid more money than you.

I realized early on that bringing a question to a boss does not make me look good. It makes me seem annoying. What bosses want are solutions to problems. They want things figured out without them. Then, once it's all figured out, or close to being figured out, they just want the opportunity to have the solution run past them in case they have anything to add.

This is where the next piece of advice comes in:

Put words in people's mouths...then let them have a chance to edit them.

On a regular basis, when I was a junior employee, I would write entire emails that answered various questions to the best of my abilities. I would even highlight the lines that I completely made up but I knew the structure of the sentence was at least correct. I'd say things like "Thank you for your interest in our services. We would be happy to provide you with the package you requested by XXXXX date." I'd highlight the XXXXX date and now all my boss has to do is say "Yeah…we can do that in two weeks." They do not have to figure out all the fluff words around it – they can just jump to the important parts that they need to sign off on.

This technique of writing emails with blank spots works great for small tasks but it can also be scaled up to larger assignments.

If I was struggling with a set of calculations, I would perform them in Microsoft Excel with various assumed values that I straight-up guessed. Then, when my boss would review it they would tell me what the values were that I guessed and since it was all done in Excel, everything automatically updated. I did NOT go into my bosses office and say "I don't know this value, therefore I stopped what I was doing, waited outside your office for twenty minutes and now you need to tell me the answer." Instead, I could spend an entire day figuring out as much as I could on a certain calculation problem, and all my boss had to do was fill in three or four blanks in the spreadsheet.

This works beyond the cubicle as well. If you work in construction and you can't figure out how to put something together, at least go through the mental steps of how you think it should go together. Then go grab your foreman and say "Hey boss, I was thinking I'd put A into B and then screw on C, but I'm just having trouble with how to attach D…your thoughts?"

Don't make your boss explain A through D to you. Show them that you've thought it through and you're just hung up on one small area.

SUMMARY: Don't ask your boss questions – instead, present problems with what you think the solution is and ask for input.

Three Strengths

We all have to start somewhere. When we get our first job we normally have no clue what we are doing and we fake it as best we can. Even if we've been working in our given profession for years or decades, we will still come across tasks where we feel way in over our head.

It has been my personal goal at work that I continually try to do new things and work with new people in order to grow and advance across the corporation. The problem with this though is that oftentimes I feel like I don't know what I am doing (many times I do not) and I've struggled to figure things out.

Then one day, when I was quite flustered at a new project I was working on, I sat down in a manager's office and asked for some advice. He said to me that there are three strengths that we must play to in order to succeed on any project. If you are lacking in one area, you must make up for it in the other two. If you are lacking in two areas, you must really make up for it in the third category. And if you don't have any of these three strengths, then you should admit defeat and let someone else take over.

Strength #1: Experience

This one takes time. This one cannot be learned overnight. If you have been doing a task for years or decades, you should by now know what you are doing and pretty much be able to coast. However, if you personally do not have experience there is another way to get experience – you must rely on other members of your team for their help.

Good leaders will admit when they need help and it's always a good idea to bring on someone to the team who can add years of experience. Sometimes a simple "This is how we did it back 7 years ago" is a great starting point.

Experience comes with time or leaning on / leveraging others experience. Ask yourself at the beginning of every project: "Do I have the necessary experience? Or do I need to bring someone in who does?"

Strength #2: Knowledge

The internet is a wonderful thing. Beyond that, many offices have technical libraries that are full of books that you might have a hard time finding online. When a project is starting up, it is a fantastic idea to read up on it as much as you can.

I build into the schedule/budget of each one of my projects a "Data Collection" day, which is spent by the entire team reading up as much as they can about the previous related projects.

Spend some time building your knowledge about a topic before you dive into a project – it will massively help you if you lack experience on the topic.

Strength #3: Boldness

If you lack experience, and you also lack knowledge, you're going to have to make up for it with boldness.

The best way to implement this is to bring onto your team those with the necessary experience and knowledge of the subject and let them make the informed decisions. You can encourage the team and do your best to bring the energy and positivity to the team…but make sure to get out of the way when the experts are talking. There's nothing more frustrating than someone trying to sound smart when they don't know what they're talking about.

SUMMARY: Experience, Knowledge, and Boldness – Best case scenario you have all three, but if you lack in one area you must make up for it in the others.

Gorilla George

We all make mistakes at work, especially when we are new employees. How do we learn? We must ask questions. We must make mistakes. But if we keep asking questions and keep screwing things up, we are going to be seen as the office idiot.

So how do we avoid this trap?

I got the following piece of advice from a family friend we all referred to as "Gorilla George" because of the enormous amount of hair he had that covered his entire body.

Is this relevant to the story? No, it's not. So I'll move on.

George once said to me: "Get a job somewhere. Make a ton of mistakes on purpose. Show up late, leave early, try to date the boss's daughter, and argue with the boss. Basically, be a horrible employee to the point that you get fired. Then, once you get fired, you'll know the line. Now, at the new company take what you learned at the first company and don't do it and now you'll be great at the new company!"

This advice is bad…but there's some gold hidden in there.

What I took away from it is a modified version.

You are obviously going to have questions at your new job. Instead of asking a variety of people questions, try to keep all your questions to one person, or a small group of people. It's preferable if this person doesn't even work in your department. Maybe all of your "Where do we keep the staples" type of questions are always asked to one specific administrative person who works on the other side of the office. Maybe all of your "How do we implement the calculations" type of questions is asked to that old guy that is about to retire.

By keeping your questions to a small set of people, you don't get the reputation from everyone that you never seem to know what you are doing…you do get that reputation from the two people that you keep asking questions of, but that is why it's a great idea to choose people who work in a different division or are about to retire.

SUMMARY: Consolidate your mistakes and questions to a small group of people.

Infectious

We've all been around a Downer – someone who will not stop talking about all the things that are going wrong with them and also the world.

Yes, there is famine. There is disease and death. As I'm writing this I am under self-quarantine in my home as there is a world-wide pandemic called the Corona Virus / COVID-19. I suspect that this won't fade from memory for quite some time, so even if you are reading this decades from now, you will still probably know about this virus that killed a huge number of people.

But despite all the bad news there is in the world, there are still a lot of reasons to be happy. There are many blessings that we all have.

My wife and I are both now working from home, so we have a lot of time to talk to each other. Yes, there are ups and downs. We turn on the news and we hear of more people succumbing to the disease, but we also hear of new treatments becoming available.

We hear of people calling family members and friends that they haven't reached out to in a long time. People are volunteering to go help get groceries for elderly couples who can't leave their homes. All over the world people are using social media to connect to others and even host online house parties to keep each other's spirits up.

Despite the world-wide pandemic that I am currently in while I'm writing this to you, there are still positives to be found, and that positivity is highly infectious.

SUMMARY: Remember that both positivity and negativity are infectious. You can spread both to others, so try to focus on the positive and the world will be a better place.

Leave the Room

Full Disclosure:

I'm the type of guy that likes loyalty. I've had the same best friend since I was 9 years old, worked for the same company since I graduated college, and I have a really hard time switching cellphone providers. I'm not exactly advocating that you fully adhere to the piece of advice I'm about to give you in this section – it needs to be taken lightly and implemented sparingly.

Are you ever on a team that would be absolutely lost without you? Do you have a group of friends that would never get to the party on time if you weren't the "parent" of the group? Do you have all your things figured out and you are constantly picking up the slack for others?

Well then, I have some news for you: You may need to find new coworkers and friends.

Again, please see my opening remark about loyalty. I'm not suggesting you ditch coworkers and friends on a regular basis. What I am suggesting is that there may be some toxic relationships (both professional and personal) that you need to get out of.

If you are the one teaching everyone how to do things and you are never learning, you need a new team. Maybe some teams you are on you should be the superstar, and maybe some teams you should be the worst player. My point is that you need to at least occasionally be the worst player so that you can be built up and learn from others.

When you are the smartest person in the room, you are actually kinda the dumbest person in the room because you are not learning or advancing.

The same goes for friend groups. I've had friends that have needed positive influences in their life and I was there for them. Some people have needed help to quit bad habits, figure out relationships, get back into exercising, and a number of life changing moments. Good friends will be there for them and help them along their journey. I've benefitted from many friends like this as well who have helped me through tough times.

But what about that friend who is constantly messing up? If you have that one person who is terribly toxic and despite your best efforts to help them they still aren't changing, it may be time to cut them loose.

I'm a big advocate of helping people, but sometimes you need to know when to give up.

At work, and in your personal life, you need to be surrounding yourself with people that build you up, help you out, encourage you, and generally push you to be a better person. Yes, continue to hang out with "the old gang" that goes way back, but be conscious of the fact that you NEED to have positive people in your life that push you if you ever want to advance in work and life.

SUMMARY: The moment you are the smartest person in the room, you are the dumbest. Join a team or a group of friends that push you to new heights, not ones that drag you down.

Cooking Eggs

This chapter is going to get me in trouble.

You're probably the type of person that has some pretty big ideas, but you can get frustrated when the Higher Ups don't agree with you. You've got that new idea for how we can cut our costs in half, increase production, and make the quality improve at the same time, but for some reason the boss just wants to keep doing it the same old way.

Well, the same old way isn't working.

So what are you to do?

I hesitate to give this advice because it can cost people their jobs, so you really need to exercise caution when doing this: You need to break a few eggs to make an omelet.

I've pushed the boundaries throughout my career. I've got us into things that no one thought would work.

Some of my initiatives have soared to new heights. Some have crashed and burned.

I have built up enough wins under my belt that when one of my ideas is implemented and fails in a spectacular fashion, people still remember the previous success stories and all is forgiven. You have to start small and build your way up. Get a few good ideas under your belt, show that you can execute a new way of doing things, and then you can start to take bigger steps.

Have I annoyed some people along the way? You bet I have. But if I annoyed them simply because they wish they would have come up with the idea or they are mad because they don't get any credit for an idea that wasn't theirs in the first place, then that is not my problem.

Of course, I have always stayed within the bounds of all initiatives being safe, legal, and ethical. However, bending or stepping slightly outside of the company norms is the way we grow. It's going to annoy some people, and you're going to have some stern warnings here and there. In extreme cases you may even lose your job. Whatever you want to implement, you need to calculate the pros and cons and make an informed decision as to whether or not you want to go down this path.

Failure can mean the loss of income. Success can mean (as it has for me) that giant promotion.

Good luck.

SUMMARY: Take a chance and break a few eggs – you have to if you ever want to make an omelet. And also remember that it's easier to ask for forgiveness than it is to ask for permission.

Remembering

We have a lot of things to deal with. Our inbox is full, our voicemail is at its limit, and our monitor is covered in sticky tabs of "to-do" lists. The number of things we have to deal with on a regular basis can seem overwhelming.

I used to have several different ways of keeping track of all the things I had to do. The problem with having multiple systems is that things fall through the cracks. I'd have one list on my phone, another list on my computer, another list written down at my desk. I'd have text messages that I still needed to reply to, and three different email addresses with emails that I've read but I hadn't responded to.

I found that multiple lists in multiple places is a bad idea. What I needed to do was to consolidate everything into one list.

One list will allow you to cross things off when they are done and see the magnitude of how much farther you have to go to complete the list.

The list can be in categories such as "By end of day", "By end of week", or "Long-term."

The important thing is that it's in one place. When you have lists all over the place things will get missed.

People will ask you a question via email, you'll mark it as read, and you'll forget about it. Had it been added to the To-Do Master List, it is far less likely it would have been forgotten.

SUMMARY: Don't make people ask you twice. Create a list of to-dos, and don't have multiple lists all over the place. Have one list that you chip away at.

Fires

I can't count the number of times I've called someone, and they've told me "I've been putting out fires all day long."

Of course, none of these people are literal firefighters. However, each new problem they deal with certainly seems like an emergency, at least to the person who starts it. And that's just it – your emergency is not necessarily other people's emergency.

Your boss deals with a lot all day long. Your clients deal with a lot all day long. And you deal with a lot all day long. If there's ever an issue that you, your boss, and your client are all struggling with then you can bet that it will get the attention that it deserves. However, those three things coming together almost never happen.

We are preprogrammed by evolution to think that our fire is the most important fire, that everyone should stop what they are doing and help us fix our problem. The world is supposed to revolve around us, right?

My dad used to say sarcastically when we were driving somewhere and there was a lot of traffic: "Don't these people know I've got somewhere to be in a hurry?"

It's tough to slow down. It's tough to zen it out and relax. Meditation helps. Sometimes a lightbulb will go on and you will just realize that the world doesn't revolve around you.

I know for me, it's a constant struggle. Patience and humility do not come easy to me, but recognizing the problem is the first step to solving the problem.

SUMMARY: Remember that the world does not revolve around you, and your fire is not necessarily as hot as someone else's fire – we've all got fires to put out.

The Nose Job

We work in a world with other people. Even if you are all alone in a lighthouse and your only job is to go turn on the light each evening and turn it off each morning, you occasionally have to interact with the helicopter guy that drops off your food and spare lightbulbs.

None of us are alone. We are all interconnected.

Human interaction is extremely complicated. Thousands of books are written every year discussing how to deal with people.

One piece of advice I got from an uncle of mine quite early in my life: It always takes two people to create an argument. You can choose to get annoyed and you can choose to not care.

We learn from a young age that when a bully at school calls us a name the worst reaction is to give them a reaction. If you call them a name back you are giving them what they want and now they are going to escalate things. A culture of escalating arguments is what changes a verbal spat into a physical altercation and sometimes even into a gun fight.

We all need to take a chill pill and stop getting our nose out of joint.

One reason why we should stop getting our nose out of joint is because there's actually a really good chance that the person you are annoyed with did not mean anything by it and was genuinely not trying to annoy you. Think of the people who cut you off in traffic. They literally didn't even see you. They obviously are not trying to maliciously hurt you. What about the person that is texting while walking and bumps into you – they literally had no idea you existed. They were not trying to hurt you.

There's a lot of people killing other people in America with guns and a lot of it has to do with escalation. One person gets annoyed at someone and confronts them. The person being confronted gets offended that they weren't talked to politely. How on Earth do you tell someone that they are annoying without offending them? Then the yelling starts. Then someone yells louder. It continues to escalate until it comes to blows and sometimes it even comes to gun shots.

If the first person would just not get their nose out of joint, one of them wouldn't be dead and the other wouldn't be in jail.

Did a coworker send you an email or talk to you on the phone in a disrespectful way? There's a really good chance they meant nothing by it. Even if they are maliciously plotting each night ways to annoy you, you still have the power to not care. Work ends, you go home, you move on. You will not always work with angels. Some of your coworkers, bosses, or clients are going to frustrate you.

Yes, at some point you need to quit your job, but far before that you can choose whether or not you are going to let it get to you.

You have the power to be annoyed or not annoyed. Don't always assume people are out to get you – most of them are not.

SUMMARY: Don't let it be so easy for other people to rattle you. Don't get your nose out of joint at every little thing. You have the power to be annoyed or let things go.

Backup Plan

We live in a crazy world. One day everything might be just fine, and the next day the entire world might be changed.

September 10, 2001 was an entirely different world from September 11. Our lives changed forever.

At one point your company is great to work for…the next day you get an email that we've been bought out by a giant corporation. Two weeks later, half of us are getting laid off.

Do you work for a small company? You talk to the owner daily? You think everything is all cool? Well, you don't know for sure what's going on with their homelife. Maybe the boss comes in one day and announces they're getting a divorce. Their spouse wants half of everything so everyone is fired, the equipment will all be sold, and they'll get half the money.

Life can come at you really fast and change things forever. Because of this, you always always always need a backup plan. Or multiple backup plans.

I've been working from the field, working from the office, and working from home for years now. I've got a slick setup at home, and I can walk into any of our corporate offices and slide right into a routine as well. Then, in 2020, the COVID-19 virus started to infect people all over the world. By March, we were all told to work from home.

Was this a massive problem for many people? Yes, yes it was. Was this a problem for those of us that already had a backup plan? Nope – we simply plugged our computers into our dual-monitor setups at home and carried on as usual.

I don't give this example to brag – I give this example to say that we always need to be thinking about the worst case scenario and always be thinking about a backup plan.

How's your resume looking? When's the last time you updated it? When is the last time you talked to someone outside of your company, but in your same industry? Massive layoffs happen all the time – they might happen to you.

And what about outside your industry? During COVID-19, a huge number of pilots got laid off. It would be no good to them to have contacts within the airline industry – no one was hiring.

What is your diversification plan? How many pilots also know how to do XYZ? – whatever that XYZ may be.

If all your skills are all in the same area, what are you going to do if there is a worldwide crisis that affects that area?

How much money do you have in savings? What costs could you cut to make rent/mortgage payments?

People spend a lot of time watching NetFlix and caring about issues that have nothing to do with them, but they don't spend time thinking about a backup plan.

Now's the time. Think about your backup plan. Think about multiple backup plans. It might just save your life.

SUMMARY: You always need a backup plan, or multiple backup plans. It doesn't matter what the situation is – have backup plans.

Weekend Plans

Have you heard the expression "Fake it 'til you make it"? Well that expression can be applied to this chapter, although I hope you graduate out of the "faking it" school soon.

On Friday afternoon, one of the most common questions around the watercooler is: "So…any big plans for this weekend?"

And guess what? On Monday morning, around that same water cooler: "So…did you get up to anything exciting this weekend?"

Let's face it: Many of us sleep in on weekends, watch TV, do nothing that's interesting, and then go back to our jobs on Monday.

For starters, you need to at least stop saying how boring your weekend is/was. On Friday's it's perfectly acceptable to say "I'm thinking about going to go see that new movie" – you don't have to actually go, but at least it's better than saying "Nothing…how about you?"

On Monday, it'd be great if you could say that you actually did go see that movie.

Can you pump it up from there? Of course you can.

Not every single weekend has to be your own personal reality show, but it does not help you in a professional setting to have a non-existent personal life.

People want to work with people who are interesting and nice and polite and fun to be around. You can't necessarily be all those things, but you can try to be at least some of them. Doing something, anything, on the weekend or in your spare time gives people something other than work to talk about. Read a book or watch an interesting documentary and have something to say about it. Go for a hike. Start planning a cool vacation. Play a musical instrument or go watch a show. Do literally anything other than "nothing much, how 'bout you?"

SUMMARY: Always have a somewhat reasonably interesting answer to the question: "What are you planning this weekend?"

First Boss

I once got some fantastic advice from my very first boss. I was working as a junior structural engineer who primarily did site inspection. I would drive around town to various construction sites and make sure that the steel reinforcing bar was the right size, length, amount, and orientation as what the engineering drawings said. If there was a problem that I couldn't easily figure out right then and there, I gave the boss a call.

I also did a little bit of design work in the office and I even helped out with general administrative tasks. It was my very first engineering job and I was eager to learn and also please my coworkers. My boss one day said to me: "Grant, always have a good answer to these three questions:

1) What have you got accomplished so far?
2) What are you currently working on?
3) What are you wanting to get done?

That advice has stuck with me my entire career. It serves two purposes. First, it keeps you out of trouble with your superiors. At any point, you know what you've done, where you are, and where you're going. If asked what's holding you back, you have an answer ready. It's a non-jerky way of bragging about all the things you've accomplished and shows your boss you've got things under control.

Second, it actually helps you get things done. It's a way of doing a self-check to see if you are on track. You don't have to just apply these three questions to your 9-5 job – you can easily ask it in a broader sense to your life.

What have you accomplished in life? What are you currently trying to accomplish? Where are you going? Do you want to be going there? What can you do to change it?

SUMMARY: Always have an answer to the three questions of: What have you got done so far?; What are you currently working on?; and What do you want to get done?

Emotional Intelligence

Do yourself a favor and read at least three books about Emotional Intelligence. I can't begin to summarize in this chapter all there is to learn in the many books written on the subject.

...but I'm going to attempt to.

Emotional Intelligence, or "EI" for short, is usually broken down into a variety of people skills. The five I'll start with are:

1 – Self Awareness:

Do you know your own strengths? Are you honest with yourself about what your own strengths actually are? Conversely, what are your weaknesses? Don't say "I care too much", "I'm a perfectionist", or "I'm just too awesome." If you're in that category you're probably mispronouncing those words. I think you meant to say "I'm super anal", "I'm annoyed if it's not done my way", and "My ego is unjustified."

But seriously – give yourself an honest evaluation of your own strengths and weaknesses, what drives you, what are your values, and how do you impact others. Do you need to change? Then change.

2 – Self Regulation:

How well can you control your tendency to do the thing you know is wrong? Maybe it's drinking and drugs, or maybe it's spouting off at the mouth during meetings when you know you should keep your mouth shut. Can you control or redirect troublesome impulses and moods?

3 – Motivation:

Money can motivate us, but can you motivate yourself and relish achievement for its own sake? Sometimes people don't want to do anything unless there's something in it for them. Can you get things done when there isn't an obvious reward?

4 – Empathy:

I once saw a cartoon drawing that described the difference between sympathy and empathy.

In one cartoon, there's a guy down in a deep dark hole, sitting with his head down. A man comes up to the edge of the hole, looks down and yells "Wow. Sure is dark down there. I'm sorry to hear that." Above the cartoon it says "Sympathy."

The next cartoon has a different man. He walks up to the hole. He looks down. He walks away. He comes back with a ladder. He puts the ladder down into the hole. He climbs down into the hole. He sits down beside the distraught fellow and puts his arm around him. Above the cartoon it says "Empathy."

Are you actually understanding other people's struggles? Do you know what they are going through? Are you putting yourself in their shoes? Or are you just saying "I'm sorry to hear that."

5 – Social Skills:

How well do you build rapport with your coworkers? There's a line in the movie *Fight Club* where the antagonist Marla says to the protagonist "Do you ever get the feeling people aren't ever actually listening to you but they are just waiting for their turn to talk?" Do you do this? Stop doing that.

SUMMARY: Read more books to help develop your Emotional Intelligence.

Section Seven:
Leadership

Politics, Law, Psychology, and Babysitting

It doesn't matter what your job is, or what training that you have – at some point you will have to do something that is outside of your area of expertise.

Are you a mechanic? Do you run a factory? Even if you are stationed at a lighthouse in the middle of nowhere, at some point you are going to have to interact with other people – and human-to-human interactions are more complicated than advanced particle physics.

My formal training is in engineering. I took multiple math, physics, chemistry, and general engineering courses. However, after a few years in Corporate America, I realized that I should have also taken courses in Politics, Law, Psychology, and probably even a Baby-Sitting course.

Politics:

I'm not talking about Republican vs. Democrat, or the history of the Whigs and the Tories. What I'm talking about is the internal jostling for power positions in the office politics world.

And if you don't work in an office, don't even try to tell me that there aren't office politics on the job site. I started my career in construction and I know that there is as much, if not more, gossip and political in-fighting between the lunchroom and the tower crane as there is between the breakroom and the boardroom.

There are many great books I'd suggest that deal with office politics. The first, is the obviously named *"Harvard Business Review: Guide to Office Politics."* This simple 170 page long book says right on the cover that it will teach you how to "Rise above the rivalry, avoid power games, and build better relationships."

Another great book is by Amy Cooper Hakim called *"Working with Difficult People."* Not only does this book give you a number of tips and tricks for how to handle that jerk in the office, it may be eye-opening for you, as you may realize that you are jerk #4 that this book talks about.

Law:

I'm not suggesting that you become a lawyer. I'm also not suggesting that you read *Black's Law Dictionary*. However, a general understanding of law will help you if you are ever seeking to run your own business or lead a department/division at work.

A simple law book that is very digestible to us non-lawyers is "*Practical Law of Architecture, Engineering, and GeoScience*" by Brian M. Samuels and Doug R. Sanders.

Don't let the title scare you. Whether you are in these industries, or you are opening up a cake-decorating company, this book lays out the basic concepts of contracts, corporations vs. sole proprietorship, suing and being sued, and other useful topics that anyone in business should be familiar with.

Psychology:

You are going to deal with people. People have feelings and opinions and a whole host of problems to deal with. It's my belief that a course in basic psychology should be mandatory for anyone entering the workforce, or even the world.

Dale Carnegie's "*How to Win Friends and Influence People*" has been a classic since its original publishing in 1936. Over 30 million copies have been sold, making it one of the bestselling books of all time.

Baby Sitting:

When I was a teenager, I volunteered at summer camps and various kids' clubs. Now that I work in Corporate America, many of the same behaviors of those kids I see in 50-year-old executives…sometimes worse versions.

If you ever have the chance to volunteer with kids, I highly suggest it. Not only does it selflessly give you a chance to give back to the community, but it selfishly gives you a free course in dealing with the emotions of youngsters – something that will come in handy during the next boardroom argument.

SUMMARY: Gain knowledge in politics, law, psychology, and babysitting.

Rick and Morty

There's a popular cartoon show the kids are watching these days called "Rick and Morty." It centers around Rick, a genius scientist, and his not-so-smart grandson, Morty. They go on various adventures around the universe in Rick's spaceship and get into all sorts of predicaments.

There's one scene I happened to catch when I was watching late night television where Rick is at the wedding of his intergalactic best friend, "Bird Person" (yes, the show is as ridiculous as it sounds).

Rick stands up to start giving a toast to the bride and groom and his opening line goes something like this:

"Look, I um…I'm not a very nice person. Because being nice is what stupid people do to hedge their bets."

That line hit me.

I love that line because of what the opposite version of it could say; that would be:

"Being mean is what smart people do because they can."

I'm sure you've met people at work that are very nice and polite…and fairly useless to work with.

There's a possibility that they are being nice because they naturally want to be nice, but there's also a very good possibility that they know that if they are liked in the company it's less likely they will get fired for poor performance.

While I could address an underperforming employee, I'd rather focus on the winners who fall into the category of Rick. They are smart, and because they are smart, they don't exactly feel the need to be a nice person.

If you are reading this book you are probably a fairly smart person. Studies show that the people who need the most amount of help don't tend to seek it out, and those that are well on their way to success are the ones who pick up the self-help books like this one.

Let's assume for a moment that you are in the "smart" category. Are you also in the "nice" category?

Do you use your position at work, your intelligence, your power, your wealth, your fame, your success to stomp on people?

I've known a number of very very smart people who let you know how dumb you are and try to make you feel stupid in front of others. They are correct in the content of what they are saying regarding what the solution to the problem is. They are also absolutely indispensable to the company because their name is on the patent – we can't get rid of them if we tried.

So unfortunately, they fall into the category of Rick. They are smart, and they know that they can be a jerk to people and everyone will just have to take it.

Do NOT be like them.

You were once stupid. You were once young and didn't know what you were doing. Just because you are now the boss or the Project Manager this does not give you the right to be rude to people. I've met people who are one person when they talk to their boss, and they turn into a completely different person when they talk to their subordinates.

SUMMARY: Don't be a jerk. Just because you are smart or the boss does not mean you have to be mean about it.

Jack Welch

If you haven't read *"Winning"* or *"Jack: Straight from the Gut"* by Jack Welch, put this book down right now (please come back to it) and add both of them to your Amazon basket.

Jack Welch was the CEO of General Electric from 1981 to 2001. He was the youngest CEO in the company's history and took the company from a $14 billion valuation to an incomprehensible $410 billion valuation – something absolutely unheard of in his time. When he left GE, he was given a $417 million severance package (the largest such payment in business history) and stayed on as an outside advisor until his death on March 1, 2020. He left behind not only his bestselling books, but also started the *Jack Welch Management Institute* – an MBA program that has been widely regarded as rivaling those of Harvard, Stanford, and MIT.

One section of Jack's books that stuck with me was the "Four E's" that is, the four things that he and other executives look for in managers that make them hand out promotions. On the other hand, if managers do not have these four E's, they need to either fix the areas that they are lacking in, or they need to "pursue options outside of this company" – a nice way of saying "You're fired!"

The first E: Energy.

You have had bosses with good energy. This does not mean they are bouncing off the walls and always smiling. You can be an introvert and quietly go about your business while still having good energy. You don't even need the good energy to be positive energy. "I'm sorry to report, but the results came back negative" is the very definition of negative…but there are ways to say things and body language and tone of voice that can still keep it being good energy.

A manager that is on the path to success leads their team with good energy. They have open and honest conversations with their team members and certainly can dish out criticism. But when it is done in a respectful, direct, and professional manner, it can still exude good energy.

The Second E: Energize.

Now I know what you are thinking: "What's the difference between good energy and Energizing?"

Just because you have good energy, does not mean that it is contagious to your team. If your energy is consistently good but there are a few members on your team that have bad energy, you may need to change things up. This is a great opportunity to have a one-on-one conversation with them as to how they are feeling. Maybe they have a loved one at home that is dealing with health issues and if they could work from home to care for them (maybe just one day a week) this would make them a lot happier. Maybe there is some other small area that can be improved but it won't be improved unless you investigate it a bit. Many people will be receptive to talking about their issues and problems if you specifically ask them, but don't expect them to come to you without being provoked.

You may have good energy, but if your team does not, you need to do something to fix it. Oftentimes that can be as easy as having a simple conversation.

The Third E: Edge.

What sets you apart from others? What is your edge? I guess Jack could have used the word "Differentiator" but then he wouldn't get to stick with the "E" theme.

You should consider taking an online course, getting a certificate, doing a weekend course, or taking an exam to make you a certified something who is an "expert" in a certain area. If you aren't an expert, you at least took some course or read some book on a topic that now gives you an edge over the competition.

Of course, taking a course costs money, takes time, and you might actually fail the test and not become certified. It is difficult to pass tests – if it isn't difficult then the results won't be very impressive.

A very easy way to have an edge over the competition is to simply be willing to do things that others are not.

From a customer point of view, do you offer home deliveries when your competition does not? Do you offer 24/7 customer service when your competition's call centers are only open 9-5 eastern time? What can you do in your business (even if it's small) that gives you an edge over the competition?

From an internal competitive perspective, how do you stack up to your coworkers? I'm not a fan of the Hollywood backstabbing path up the corporate ladder. Rather, if you can find and edge that makes you look good and doesn't make others look bad, then you are golden.

A very simple one (especially for young employees) is to be willing to do things that others think is beneath them. I can't tell you the number of times I've washed the dishes in the breakroom, fixed the photocopier, put more paper in the photocopier, unjammed a stapler, replaced a lightbulb, lit the candles on a coworker's birthday cake, held the door open for the entire office as we all returned from a lunch meeting, stayed in the office late to print off the reports for tomorrow, etc. etc.

Are these tasks for a "Junior" employee, maintenance person, or an administrative assistant? Of course they are. However, thinking that things are beneath you is a horrible way to go through life. You don't need to constantly be doing junior-level tasks, but someone has got to do it, and if you have the know-how to do it, it doesn't hurt you.

I remember we once hired someone who, on their first day, asked "Who does the photocopying around here?" The response was "We don't have a specific person that does that – everyone does their own."

She quit that afternoon.

The final E is: Execute.

I've had bosses who had great energy, energized their team, and had a distinct advantage that put them ahead of everyone…but they failed to ever actually get things done. They could not execute.

Pontificating about the project and about how a company should be run is a great way to write a book. It is not a great way to lead a team.

At the end of the day, the job needs to get done. We need to ship the product, deliver the report, finalize the projections, install the device, or build the component.

SUMMARY: Every manager must have good energy, energize their team, have a competitive edge, and execute the deliverable.

Getting Results

You've tried everything, you've followed all the check lists, and you are still not getting results.

I'm a guy that likes lists. I like going through the various "Roadblocks to success" or "Reasons why you fail" lists and see if I am doing any of them.

No list is perfect, and I recognize that this book is essentially a giant list of things people should be doing to achieve "success."

Here's another check list to run through if you are still not finding the results that you desire on a given project:

Vision:

Big ideas need a goal to shoot for and the team needs to know what the end-goal is. We can't aimlessly start something and have no idea what the big picture is. What are we trying to build? What do we think it's going to look like when it's done? We might not ever get to where we originally planned on going, but if we don't at least start with a vision of the future, then we shouldn't be shocked when we never get there.

Plan:

Plans can be boring, but they need to be done.

If you're not a person who plans things out step-by-step, then add someone to your team who does. Find a "Details Person" or, as you may call them "That guy who is super annoying."

Well, he may be annoying, but he is essential. You need to have a plan that lays out where you are going and the various steps that need to be taken along the way.

Drive:

This one is tough. Upper Management can stomp on your ideas and not approve things until they see results. How can you show results to something that hasn't even started yet?

Drive is something that you need to find deep within yourself to keep yourself going when others said you can't.

I love climbing mountains and consider myself a bit of an amateur mountaineer. I once had the opportunity to climb Mt. Rainer with Dave Hahn. Dave has the world record for the most successful Mount Everest Summits from a non-Sherpa. He has attempted the summit of Everest 21 times and made it to the top 15 times. He found the body of George Mallory after it had been missing since 1924, and he has also climbed Mt. Rainer over 270 times. He is a force of nature and also an incredibly humble guy to be around.

While climbing Mt. Rainer, he said something to the team that has really stuck with me: "I'm not your cheerleader. I will never push you to the top. I will definitely tell you to turn around and go home, but I won't push you to the top. You need to push yourself to the top."

Drive is something that comes from within. One person can read a self-help book and become driven, another person can read a self-help book and become discouraged. It's my hope that you can find drive within yourself to do the thing you want to do…but ultimately that one is on you.

Patience:

Good things come to those who wait.

Even if you've done all the right things, you are still going to have to wait for the idea to work out. Sometimes this takes hours, days, weeks, months, years, or decades.

Sometimes it never happens.

I have started many ideas only for them to fizzle out.

I've started ideas to have them finally be executed a long time later.

There's no time machine, so you just must sometimes wait to see how the chips fall.

SUMMARY: Vision with a Plan, plus Drive, plus Patience, equals Results.

Who's Responsible?

When things are going well, everyone seems to want to take the credit. When shit hits the fan, everyone seems to want to point fingers and shift the blame.

A mentor of mine once that told me that "Responsibility" is the combination of two things: Duties and Rights.

"Rights" is what everyone wants to cling to. When the sale is made, the person responsible has the right to celebrate and get the praise.

When we are deciding on a new venue for this year's Christmas party, the person responsible has the right to pick out the place that they want.

"Rights" are awesome. We all want them.

However, if that person is responsible and they have all the rights, they must also realize that they have duties as well.

When we lose the sale, it's their duty to figure out what went wrong, how we can fix it for next time, and take the blame for the failure.

When the venue is picked and it turns out to be too small and overpriced, it's that same person's duty to find a new venue ASAP.

I've seen it far too often that people clamor over each other to become responsible for something when really what they just want is all the rights and none of the duties.

A true leader recognizes that with rights, comes duties, and this is the essence of "Responsibility."

SUMMARY: Remember that when you are "Responsible" for something that not only gives you the right to make decisions, but it also gives you the duties that come along with it. Responsibility equals rights+duties.

Leadership

Of all the business books written I think "Leadership" is the topic that is most discussed.

Am I the writer who finally cracks the code and summarizes "What is leadership" into a single chapter? My ego may be large, but it's not that large. This chapter will give you my definition of leadership to not serve as the definitive definition, but rather to add to the pile of all the other writers who have tackled this task.

Here goes:

"Leadership is the ability to get people to grow and/or succeed."

Yelling at someone to get them to do something is not leadership. They didn't grow as a person, and forced labor is not success. Some forms of forced labor are physical – think the classic definition of slavery complete with whips and chains. But many other forms of forced labor are also slavery.

"If you don't do this, you're fired" is slavery. You have bills to pay, the economy is tough right now, so if you get fired you can't pay your bills and then you can't eat. It's less direct than a whip literally hitting you, but it's still punishment for not complying with an order from a boss. You are a slave to your boss because they give you money and money gives you food. It's a longer path to follow, but it's still slavery.

When a boss threatens you with job loss, they are not being a leader – they are being a slave master.

Wayne Gretzky is widely considered to be the greatest hockey players of all time. However, there are arguments to the contrary. Some people believe he played in a watered-down league, he was propped up by an all-star team, and people simply played more minutes and scored more goals back in his era. But even the biggest haters of Gretzky have to admit that his stats are off the chart. When compared with any other player Gretzky stands in a category all by himself.

After he retired from playing, Gretzky started coaching. It did not go well. He was quoted as once saying "Can't you guys just do what I used to do?"

Being amazingly awesome at something, as Gretzky was, does not mean you are going to be able to transfer your skills to others. You are not necessarily going to have the ability to get others to grow and succeed. In fact, pretty much all of the best leaders in the NHL (the coaches) they themselves were pretty terrible players. A good player is not necessarily a good coach and a good performer is not necessarily a good leader.

When thinking if you fit the qualities of a leader you certainly can read any of the hundreds of books written on leadership. If you want a more manageable list, I've picked out my favorite 10 books on the subject at:

www.SelfTaughtMBA.com/leadership-and-motivation.html

SUMMARY: If you are trying to become a leader, ask yourself if you are able to get other people to grow and/or succeed. If you aren't, then those are skills you need to work on and can be found by reading more books on leadership.

Mushroom Management

A lot of advice books are about how to deal with X type of person. *Working with Difficult People* by Amy Cooper Hakim has tips and tricks for how to navigate tricky personalities in the workforce.

However, instead of giving you tips and tricks for how to work with certain types of people / styles of management, I'd rather point out some jackass moves and let you look in the mirror. Are you the difficult person no one can stand? Do you do a type of management style that is crap? Here are some common types of management styles that you need to ask yourself if you do, and if you do them, then you need to stop right now.

Mushroom Management

This style of management is when you as the boss divvy out tasks to your team members and don't give anyone any context. They don't know the end goal, they aren't told the vision or the final objective. You give them small bite-sized tasks and no one sees how it all fits together. Employees at the company are not told about the big idea.

This is called "Mushroom Management" because employees, much like mushrooms, are kept in the dark and fed bullshit.

Don't practice this style of management.

Seagull Management

You may have had a manager that is a big talker. They give grandiose speeches and pontificate a lot. They also like putting their nose into every single detail. The critique everything that everyone is doing, and not in a helpful way. Finally, they are often there for one moment, and then gone, without any warning. Maybe they take every Friday off, but they don't actually tell anyone this formally.

This is called "Seagull Management" because, much like a seagull, these managers make a lot of noise, shit on everything, then fly away.

Don't practice this style of management.

Pigeon Management

Pigeon Management is almost the same as Seagull Management. They also make a lot of noise, they also shit on everything, but instead of flying away, they sit there and watch you for hours.

Don't practice this style of management.

Cat Management

This one is pretty self-explanatory.

A cat manager ignores their employees.

Don't practice this style of management.

SUMMARY: Don't do the following things to you staff: Keep them in the dark about the big picture, shit on their ideas, or straight-up ignore them.

Section Eight:
Running a Company

ENRON: Behavior vs. Performance

In an interview conducted in front of MBA students, GE's legendary CEO, Jack Welch, said that all companies can put their employees somewhere on a graph that is broken into four quadrants, with "Behavior" on one axis and "Performance" on the other axis. Where the majority of companies place their employees will determine if you are a good company, or if you are the definition of an evil company: ENRON.

Let's start with someone that has high behavior and high performance. Everyone loves this person. They are a joy to be around. Their personal behavior in the office and the way they treat others is spectacular. Last month, they remembered that it was Sally's anniversary and not only did they bring in donuts for the whole team, they wrote a silly song about Sally and performed it in front of the team. Everyone laughed.

Not only does this person score high on the behavior metric, their sales are through the roof. It's amazing how many customers they bring in and they continue to close the sale.

What happens to someone in this category? They get promoted. They get a raise and a bonus.

We are not worried about them.

The second category are people that have high behavior but poor performance. This is the guy in the office that everyone loves, but he just can't seem to do his job right.

What happens to this guy? Well, a lot of the times he gets coached. A lot of times he realizes what he is doing wrong and makes the necessary change. With a little luck, and some change of tactics, he might move into the High Behavior / High Performance category.

Of course, sometimes, there isn't a lot of leniency and employees like this get laid off.

The third category is someone who is a jerk and also can't do their job. They are low behavior, low performance.

What happens to them? Well, unless they are the boss's son, they don't last long. They might be given a few chances to change, but you can't always teach an old dog new tricks. Usually, they are fired.

All this seemed pretty straight forward, and I wasn't overly interested as Jack was explaining it until he got to the fourth and final category.

This is the category of people who are complete jerks…but they get things done. They have low behavior but yet they have high performance.

These are the people who are mean to coworkers, but polite to customers and always make the sale. They belittle their subordinates but suck up to their boss. They are professional in the boardroom but tell off-color jokes in the breakroom. And in extreme cases, they are sticklers for other people following the rules, but when you dig into their finances, they themselves are bending or straight up breaking the rules, or maybe even the laws.

What should happen to these types of people?

Jack Welch states that in a good company, bad behavior is treated like bad performance. It needs to be addressed, given a chance for reform, and if there's no change, then this type of person needs to be fired.

But what happens when people with bad behavior but AMAZING performance not only don't get fired but they get promoted? You get yourself ENRON – the worst company in Corporate American history.

Outside of Corporate America, there are many other examples of low behavior but high performance being not only tolerated but also celebrated. Think of the athlete that cheats on his wife but he continues to win championships, the boxer who beats his wife but continues to dominate in the ring, or the singer who sells out stadiums but routinely is arrested on drug-related charges.

SUMMARY: Do not tolerate bad behavior, even if it's from a high-performer…unless you want to become ENRON, a cheater, a wife-beater, or a drug addicted criminal.

Internal, External, Technological

Why did we go to school? Why did we take the training course? Why did we work under Bob for two years to learn all that we know how to do?

Generally, if we have a job, we spent some amount of time learning how to do it. Some of us take years of post-secondary training, or some of us learn on the job and figure it out by YouTube videos. Regardless of how we got to where we are, we have technical challenges that we face each day…or at least we are supposed to face each day.

Unfortunately, the external problems of dealing with filling out forms for the government just so we can do our job, or dealing with customers who just don't understand that this product isn't even supposed to do the things they are asking for, can oftentimes take up more of our day than the technical problems that we are supposed to face.

This book cannot teach you nor give you advice on how to solve your technical problems. That book would be as large as an entire library. However, there are many external problems that have many of the same characteristics.

Let's start with the external problem of the government.

Why on earth do we have to fill out this form? There are so many forms to fill out and hoops to jump through in order for us to be in compliance with the regulations.

You can vote for a politician who claims they are going to cut red tape (they all claim this) and you can canvas your local representative to get some of the red tape bypassed. Good luck with that.

My approach is to view it as a board game, or video game. We are all playing by these BS rules and we all have to fill out the same forms. Your competitor has to deal with getting the product approval letter just like you do. Treat it as if it's just another step that you have to go through. Maybe even train a different employee and leverage their skills to get the form filled out, with your help.

The second type of external problem is generally the customer. The customer does not necessarily know what they need or want but they can convince themselves that they do.

Dealing with difficult customers takes patience and tact. But sometimes you just have to let one of them go.

You will struggle with some bad customers. It's your job to keep your cool, but also know when to hang up the phone or physically walk away.

We are trained how to handle technological problems. We deal with and are frustrated with external problems. However, the biggest hurdle is often internal struggles. You need to get your boss to talk to their boss to talk to their boss to get approval for the new thing. Good luck.

In large corporations, there are so many levels of management that it is a wonder why anything ever gets accomplished. Projects cost millions if not billions of dollars because there are sometimes dozens of people working on the project charging to it who all need to have their say and give their approval. People don't want to rock the boat for fear of being laid off, so they are unwilling to approve outside the box ideas.

I saw a cartoon once of a boss sitting across from a subordinate and the caption read "We love this new innovative idea…unfortunately it's never been tried before so we won't be implementing it."

Some companies encourage outside-the-box thinking. Many do not. It is the companies that stifle employees creativity and require far too many levels of approval that eventually get swallowed up by leaner companies that celebrate individual creativity.

SUMMARY: We are prepared for technological challenges, we can figure out external challenges and even enjoy them if we treat them like a game, but the real challenge is to kill off unnecessary levels of internal approvals that slow innovation.

Creating Change

Have you ever tried to implement a change at your company, but it just can't seem to get off the ground?

There are so many obstacles for real change that it can often seem impossible to even know where to start.

Who do I need to ask permission to for this to get approved? What happens if we start, get halfway through, and the whole thing gets cancelled?

I struggled to implement a new program at my company until I came across "The five elements of a successful change."

In this chapter, I'll lay out what happens when just one of the five elements is missing, and show that when you have all five it will in all likelihood become a success.

Confusion:

Let's say that your plan has people on the team with the skills to get the job done. It also has incentives for a successful implementation. Upper Management has given you the proper resources to implement the change (usually this is a charge code for you to buy the new thing or pursue the new technique) and you have an action plan of what needs to happen.

But still you fail.

Why?

Because you lacked an overall vision.

When a team is gathered together and you are assigning tasks, no one is going to know where we are going unless you tell them.

Is the new product going to be in every office? Is the new technique for installing the thing going to revolutionize the way we do business around here? If there's no long-term vision, people can't get on board and it's just another set of tasks that they will lacklusterly follow or not follow through on altogether.

Anxiety:

What happens when you have the Vision, Incentives, Resources, and Action Plan, but are missing skills?

Anxiety.

You need people on the team with the technical skills to get the job done. You can have the other four elements of a successful change, but if no one has the skills to actually do the thing you are trying to do, you will fail.

Resistance:

You've got Vision, Skills, Resources, and an Action Plan...but you are lacking Incentives. What will happen now is that you will face resistance.

Employees will ask "Why am I going to change? Why do I have to do it another way?" If you can't answer with any form of incentive, then you will face resistance. Will the new process save time? That is an incentive and that needs to be communicated with the team. Will the new process make things easier? That is an incentive and needs to be communicated with the team. Will this new idea bring in more business, drive up profits, and thus increase end-of-year bonuses? That is an incentive and needs to be communicated with the team.

Frustration:

Let's suppose you have a Vision, you got a team with skills, the incentives are there, and you even have a full action plan for how to implement the change.

But you don't have the resources you need.

This one is simple. You will have massive frustration.

Change needs resources. Usually that comes in the form of money.

If Upper Management wants you to change things, wants you to innovate, wants you to take things to the next level...but doesn't want to give you a charge code to do it with, you will have massive frustration and many people will give up.

False Starts:

The final combination of failed change initiatives is when you have Vision, Skills, Incentives, and Resources, but no Action Plan.

You (or a team of you) need to sit down and figure out step-by-step how the change is going to be implemented. There needs to be milestones and goals and measurable items.

You must have an Action Plan for how to implement a change.

Change:

The five elements of Change in a corporation are:

Vision, Skills, Incentives, Resources, and an Action Plan.

If you lack any of these elements, you will fail in your plan for change.

SUMMARY: The five elements of Change in a corporation are Vision, Skills, Incentives, Resources, and an Action Plan.

Safety First

"Safety is our Number One Priority."

It started in the construction industry where no one wore any personal protective equipment. People were literally dying at work on a regular basis due to zero safety standards.

Laws were passed, the industry changed, and now everyone at a job site wears every piece of personal protective equipment imaginable.

Then it continued to the office worker.

Do you sit in an office all day long? Have you ever been injured at all or know of anyone that has ever been injured? No? But do you still have to sit through a safety orientation course that lasts for hours? Of course you do. "Safety" is everywhere in Corporate America, and the way in which we approach it is making us LESS safe.

I'll break this chapter down into two categories: 1) Jobs that are dangerous and have a high probability of killing you; and 2) Office jobs that have an extremely low risk of killing you.

Construction / High Risk Jobs:

Personal protective gear such as gloves, hearing protecting, and face shields absolutely need to be worn at certain times during certain activities. The problem that I see on job sites is that every piece of PPE is required at all times, and by constantly wearing them we make ourselves less safe.

Should you wear a face shield while you are using a steel grinder and sparks are flying in your face? Of course you should. Little pieces of metal are literally flying straight at you.

But should you take it off when you are changing out a disk so you can see what you are doing? Yes, you should as well. Unfortunately, your safety manual might forbid this.

Should you wear hearing protection while you are using the grinder and it is making a very loud screaming/grinding noise? Of course you should.

But should you take out your ear plugs while you are walking to another part of the job site in order to hear someone possibly yell out "HEY MAN, DON'T WALK THERE!" Yes you should, but your safety manual might forbid this.

We've gone from a set of rules and regulations that were put in place to help people, and now instead we have too much safety and it's all about covering the company's liability in case you were hurt.

Safety on the jobsite isn't about keeping workers safe, it's about keeping corporations protected from being sued.

Office Jobs / Low Risk Jobs:

A great way to make employees stop caring and stop listening is to present safety messages to them in a manner that has no bearing on their real life.

Safety in an office should be kept short. There are very few things that can kill you in an office environment and by treating it like we're working in a factory that makes explosives you get employees with glazed-over eyes.

Correct posture while sitting, standing up to stretch your legs occasionally, washing your hands after using the washroom, and looking away from your computer screen – these are simple things that can actually be talked about.

Do not come up with every conceivable bad thing that could happen, otherwise employees are going to sit forever in a safety meeting and tune out.

Forms:

I hate forms.

The problem with treating safety as a liability protection is that the forms keep growing and growing because our corporate lawyer has advised us that we need to cover all our bases.

If we truly cared about safety, the forms that we fill out and the safety checklists would be kept to one page maximum.

I've spent a lot of my career working on a jobsite and I've served on our company's safety committee.

While on the committee, I summarized the 50-page long on-site safety checklist and created a one-page version.

People can read one page. People can discuss one page. It's easily digestible and understandable.

When safety forms are too long, no one reads them – they just flip to the end and sign it. They are not safe, and they've signed their life away to the corporation.

Safety Gear:

Finally, don't ever make employees buy their own safety gear. Safety gear should be brand new, high-quality, fashionable, comfortable, readily available, and totally free. Branding safety gear with the company logo is also a nice touch.

SUMMARY: If you're in charge of safety on a job site, make it practical and don't make people wear PPE when it actually makes them less safe. If you're in charge of safety in an office, make it applicable to an office, not a doomsday scenario. Make all forms one-page max. Finally, safety gear should be brand new, high-quality, fashionable, comfortable, readily available, and totally free.

Talk is Cheap

Some of us are selling a product and/or service, and some of us are creating that product and/or service. If you've ever worked on a team where there's a total disconnect between the sales/marketing/branding department and the operations/production team, you will know the frustration that I have dealt with.

I've worked in both departments. I've created proposals, delivered presentations to clients, and sold things. I'm going to put my bragging hat on for a moment and let you know that one year I led the office in proposal wins – I was the proposal manager for 29 pursuits and we were the successful winner of all 29 of them.

But what are sales worth if the delivery of the product is garbage?

You can only go so far with flashy presentations, slick commercials, or quick-witted, fast-talking sales personnel. Eventually, your poor product will catch up to you, your reputation will suffer, and your sales will drop.

That is why the production staff need to be personally invested in the quality of the product being delivered because ultimately if the sales drop off there will have to be layoffs that will affect everyone.

So why doesn't the production staff take as much pride in their work as the sales staff? The sales team at some companies literally have a gong that they hit to celebrate a new win. While that isn't always the case, it's practically always the case that every sales team celebrates their wins in some manner. Why doesn't the production team?

Leadership comes from the top, and Upper Management needs to let the production folks know that their work is pivotal for the company's success. When a client says "Thanks for the report, it was exactly what we were looking for" this positive review needs to be celebrated. The production staff need to feel like they are valued, and in turn they will (hopefully) put more into their work.

SUMMARY: Put the same emphasis on production as you do on sales. Celebrate good reviews, because good quality work is more important than a sales pitch and will create repeat customers.

Fishing

There's an expression used in sales "They're so good at sales, they could sell water to a fish."

This is meant as a compliment. It's meant to say that the sales team does an excellent job, their numbers are high, their customer satisfaction is fantastic. In fact, it's so fantastic that they could sell a product (water) to someone who doesn't even need it (a fish).

But take a step back – is it moral and ethical to sell a product to someone that doesn't need it?

Think of cigarettes. They literally kill you. Slick marketing is the only way those products are sold.

Think of "medicine" that you see advertised on late night TV. It's useless and will do nothing for you. Slick marketing and outright lying is the only way those products are sold.

It's universally agreed upon that cigarettes and miracle oils are evil products and no one should be proud of selling them. But does your company also sell a product or service that the client doesn't need?

When you're installing a TV system, do you try to upsell to get an in-home security system when the building already has one? Do you push for the sealant to be installed that will prolong the life of the product 50 years when it's scheduled to be torn down in 5? Do you get a client to pay for a giant study of a proposed project that you already know they have no money for?

Don't do this. Don't celebrate being able to sell services to people that they don't need. Don't sell water to a fish.

SUMMARY: Be proud of the price, quantity, and quality of what you are selling to someone. Don't pull the wool over anyone's eyes. If they don't actually need the product, don't try to upsell it to them. Don't sell water to a fish.

Four Groups of Employees

Most companies have annual reviews of their employees. I've found that there doesn't seem to be an industry-standard for how these reviews are conducted. What is the point of an annual review if it's different every year, has no follow-up, and there's not positive or negative consequences of the review?

It's my view that all employees of a company fall into four categories. Here they are:

Category #1: Keep doing what you are doing

To put a positive spin on this, employees who fall into this category are doing all the things that their boss wants them to do. Their objectives have been made clear to them and they are doing them well. They should be happy where they are at and they should just keep on keeping on.

To put a negative spin on this, employees who fall into this category are not shining stars, they simply are fulfilling the duties that they need to do. Many other people could do what they are doing, but they are doing an ok job and it's easy to just keep them there.

As a boss who is reviewing people, let them know if they are in this category and if there's anything they should do differently.

Category #2: Do More

To put a positive spin on this, employees who fall into this category deserve a raise and a promotion. They are doing a great job of managing projects that are the size of X and now they should graduate to managing projects the size of 2X…or whatever the multiplier may be.

To put a negative spin on this, employees who fall into this category need to pick things up. If they've been doing the same thing for years, why have they not taken on more responsibility? It's time for them to step up to the plate.

As a boss who is reviewing people, let them know if they are in this category and if there's anything they should do differently.

Category #3: Do Something Different

To put a positive spin on this, employees who fall into this category are doing too many things. They are good at A, B, C, D, E, and F, but really they should focus on B and C, let others do A, D, E, and F, and it would be great if they could help out the company and figure out how to do G.

To put a negative spin on this, employees who fall into this category are pretty bad at all the things they are doing, but we want to give them a chance to try something different. Maybe they were at one point great at their job, but for whatever reason they aren't so good anymore. It's time to try something different.

As a boss who is reviewing people, let them know if they are in this category and if there's anything they should do differently.

Category #4: Leave the Company

To put a positive spin on this, employees who fall into this category maybe need to retire. They have done a fantastic job and now it's time to move on and let someone else lead the show. Maybe they retire, maybe they move on to a new company, maybe they start their own company. We've loved having them on the team, and it's time for them to move on.

To put a negative spin on this, employees who fall into this category are poor at their job and need to be fired. Multiple attempts should be made to fix the problem, but eventually people need to be let go.

As a boss who is reviewing people, let them know if they are in this category.

SUMMARY: If you're a boss who gives annual reviews, put your employees into one of four categories: "Keeping doing what you're doing", "Do more of what you're doing", "Do something different", or "Leave the company."

Leap Frog

When people hear the terms "Horizontal and Vertical Integration" their eyes glaze over. What do those terms even mean?

Please stay with me here and let me attempt to explain what these terms mean and why, if you have the power to do so, you need to be fostering an environment that encourages these things.

We'll start with an example of Internal Horizontal Integration.

Let's say you work in the New York office. You are a drafter. You are struggling with how to import the new drawing into the old drawing. You know that there's a really smart drafter in the Chicago office who could probably figure this out. In a poorly integrated horizontal team structure, you would have no way of contacting that drafter directly. You first have to ask your boss to talk to his boss to then talk to him to then get back to his boss to then talk to your boss to then explain the answer to you.

What a waste of time.

In a well integrated horizontal team structure, you can pick up the phone and call him. He answers your question. It's that simple.

This might seem like a no-brainer. Why would any manager ever want to stop one office from talking to another? Well, I've worked for bosses like this. They do not want you to talk to anyone other than your boss. Everything has to go through the hierarchy.

Does this slow things down? Yes it does. Does this get the answer all jumbled up in a game of corporate telephone? Yes it does.

Companies should allow people to talk across the corporation to similar corporate levels and strip away the who-reports-to-who chain of command.

Now let's look at an example of Internal Vertical Integration.

Let's say you have an idea for a new technology that can make your company more competitive and give you a great advantage over others. However, it's pretty expensive so someone a number of corporate levels above you is probably going to have to sign off on this.

In a company that has poor internal vertical integration, you tell your boss your idea. They might hate it and kill the idea, or maybe they twist the idea around and make it bad and then pass it onto their boss. By the time it gets up to the level that it needs to get to it will either be a garbage idea or it won't even get there.

I have worked for a company that had a "Ask the CEO" section on the internal web portal. This was a direct connection from the lowest level employee to the highest. These types of feedback forms can be misused, but it is just one example of a way in which a junior employee can communicate with a senior employee.

Outside of "Ask the CEO" employees can simply email their boss's boss's boss. In poorly vertically integrated companies, your boss will flip out when you email someone above him. In well vertically integrated companies, talking to people multiple levels up the corporate ladder is encouraged. Why would we ever want to discourage communication? Steve Jobs, Bill Gates, Mark Zuckerberg and countless other titans of tech encourage interns to send them emails about new ideas – your company should be no different.

These have been examples of internal integration. External is similar, it's just on a larger scale. External integration is when one company that makes tractors buys another company that makes tractors and then they say to each other "Hey new company that we just acquired…how do you make yours so quiet? Let's integrate that technology into our tractors as well." It's the same thing, just on a larger scale.

SUMMARY: If you are in the upper management position to do so, foster an environment where employees are encouraged to communicate horizontally across the corporation with people in multiple different offices without having to go through a series of bosses. Also encourage an environment where a junior employee can bring up an idea to a senior employee who is multiple corporate levels above them.

Cannibals

Steve Jobs once said "Don't be afraid to cannibalize yourself. If you don't, someone else will."

His advice is true. The invention of the iPhone destroyed the sales of the iPod. The iPad has hurt laptop sales.

If you are in a product-centered industry and you work in R&D, you always need to think about how you can make a new product that can destroy your old ones. You will receive pushback. You will work with people who worked on that last "Next great thing" and you are now pushing for a device that will make it irrelevant. They might take it personally. That's not your problem

In a product-based world your competitor is always trying to steal your ideas, build on them, make them better, package them as their own, and steal away your sales. You should be doing the same thing.

SUMMARY: Don't be afraid to cannibalize your products. If you don't, your competitor will.

The Art of War

In 500 B.C. ancient Chinese military strategist Sun Tzu wrote *The Art of War*. Still to this day it is required reading for tank commanders in the US Military.

The English translation is widely regarded as one of the most important books in literature, and this line in particular stood out to me: "In happiness at overcoming difficulties, people forget the danger of death."

This is the reason why soldiers are allowed to listen to their own music mix in their ears while they are killing their targets. Their duties are much more enjoyable when there's a bumping soundtrack to listen to.

This ancient advice has implications for the corporate world as well.

When there's a particularly difficult task for the office to do, are you doing your best as a manager to make it enjoyable? When the group is pulling an all-nighter to get the document finished on time, do you go out and buy everyone pizza? – and the good type of pizza, not that crappy place around the corner.

Are employees being thanked and praised and rewarded? Everyone likes being recognized for their hard work.

Work can be tough. Work can be a grind. However, if you are in the position to oversee people, you need to ask yourself if you are trying your best to maintain happiness throughout the team. If you don't know how to do that, then management is maybe not the position you should be in.

SUMMARY: Foster an environment of happiness at work.

Machiavelli

The 16th century Italian diplomat by the name of Niccolò Machiavelli wrote *"The Prince."*

You may have heard the phrase "He's acting in a pretty Machiavellian way" which means the person is being manipulative.

That comes from this book. It's essentially a 1-2-3 guide to being a terrible person and manipulating your way to the top. Many CEOs and politicians love the book, although they would never admit it publicly.

In the opening chapters, Niccolò touches on a subject that I see as a systemic problem across Corporate America. He says: *"A wise prince ought to adopt such a course that his citizens will always in every sort and kind of circumstance have need of the state and of him, and then he will always find them faithful."*

We see this with people who create a job so complicated that only they know how to do it and they then make themselves "unfireable."

I knew an IT guy that knew passwords to the old servers and refused to tell anyone. We had migrated onto new servers but every month or so there was a need to pull up the old data. Not only was he the only person that knew the passwords, he was the only person who understood FORTRAN, the computer language that was needed to boot up the system. He could not be fired because he was the only person who could access the old files.

This is corporate hijacking and should be illegal, but it is not.

I've met accountants that had access to the internal software system that I had to ask how we were doing on certain budget items. I know that they are given the read/write permissions to the internal systems because they have been trained on what to do in there and we can't have just anyone poking around. There's sensitive information such as employee salaries easily accessed from inside the system.

I, however, knew all the salaries of every person working on the project because I worked as a Project Management Analyst and it was my job to check in on budgets and schedules. I can understand if they didn't want to give me write permissions, but refusing to give me read permissions was simply a way of them justifying their position.

Luckily, the Senior Project Leader agreed that I should be given access to see inside the system. An inefficiency was deleted and I was now able to do my job faster.

I understand that people want to protect their jobs, but when your job is solely to think up creative reasons to keep your job...you shouldn't have your job.

SUMMARY: Make sure every job is needed. If your job is to think up creative ways as to why you need to keep your job, then I'm sorry, but you should not have a job.

Hoop Jumping

It's an unfortunate reality of the world that we live in that there are a lot of hoops to jump through. Are they pointless? A lot of the time they are. Can we do anything to change them? Sometimes we can, usually we can't. We just need to learn how to play the game and jump through those hoops.

There was once a Senator who had two properties. One was a quaint little cabin in the woods that his family had owed for years. The other was a large downtown townhome that he was paying a mortgage on. The rules of the Senate state that if you are from a city outside of the capitol and it's not reasonable for you to commute in each day, you are allowed to expense your second home in the capitol.

This particular Senator had been living in the capitol for years, but since he had a family home hundreds of miles away, he claimed that as his "Primary Residence" and the fancy place in the city was his "Secondary Home."

The taxpayers paid his mortgage, property taxes, and utility bills for years before someone caught one.

He resigned and there was a giant investigation. As a result of the criminal case, he was found innocent. He was following the rules of the Senate. He wasn't exactly following the spirit of the law, but he was following the letter of the law.

Because of this, all travel or living expenses that will be paid for by the government on a federal contract need to now go through multiple levels of approvals before you submit the receipts.

I had a project where I was going to be inspecting hiking trail bridges in the middle of nowhere. My coworker and I would drive to a rural parking lot, put on our heavy hiking backpacks that were full of food, clothing, and all inspection/camping gear, then we spent 7 straight days in the forest, drinking water from the streams we came along when we would inspect the nearby bridges.

I, as the Project Manager, had to fill out a travel form. I had to list where we would be staying each night. It's pretty ridiculous but I had to put down things like "Sleeping in a tent. Location: The forest. Address: The forest. Reason why not sleeping at home? Because I don't live in the forest."

Each day we ate camp food. Dried fruit, freeze-dried meals, crackers – normal camping food. Were we allowed to submit receipts from the store to get reimbursed? No. The rule is that everyone who works for the government gets a preset amount of money for each day of working away from home. That amount was $96.50.

Now, if you spend $20 on a breakfast at the fancy hotel you're staying at, $35 for lunch, and $40 for dinner, that $96.50 makes a lot of sense. I can see businesspeople and members of our government spending that amount of money and it not be considered insane. But here we were, eating freeze-dried meals and drinking water from the stream. Our daily meal price per person was probably $8. However, because there's no box to check that says "Giving us $96.50 is a waste of taxpayer money" we have to get the mandated per diem amount.

Sometimes we'll have clients that never seem to care about the quality of the work or what the actual report says; they just care that the correct charge code was used. I put down GH405.863 when it should have been GH405.862. Does that matter at all and will it change the content of the report? No it won't, but they are very concerned as to what budget it gets charged to. The things that we concern ourselves with sometimes never line up with what our client is concerned about.

At work you'll have system "upgrades" and now you have to fill out a different form to submit your weekly timesheet. What was wrong with the last system? Nothing. Someone just wanted to change it.

Hoops and more hoops you will constantly face as you work in Corporate America or if you ever have to do anything with the government. We are making our systems more and more complicated and it's not doing anyone any favors.

When I first moved to Colorado, I drove my truck here. It took me 5 visits to the DMV before I had my truck fully imported and registered here.

At first, they wanted to see my import papers. I drove it here from out of state and no one ever gave me any, so I had to drive to the airport and "pretend" that I had just imported it on a plane and the Customs and Border Patrol Officers had to inspect it and give me official import papers. It was manufactured in 2012 but it was sold to me as a 2013 model. 2013 and newer vehicles are exempt from air pollution testing. I had to show some paperwork that said it was a 2013 model so I would be exempt from the testing. Paperwork got lost during the whole process and it took me about 2 months to legally and properly import a vehicle to Colorado.

There are more and more forms to fill out every day in America and it slows down progress. I hope there are people high ranking in their organizations that are reading this book and have the power to change things. I hope government officials read this book and have the power to change things. New regulations are fine, but do they replace an old regulation? Is there a way to combine multiple regulations into one catch-all?

Throughout my career, I've helped to write Environmental Regulations for various construction projects. I would start with a template from a previous job. I would come across something that said *"The contractor is to refrain from depositing either intentionally or unintentionally any materials into the watercourse or the surrounding areas that may contain but are not necessarily limited to: Toxic gases, poisonous chemicals, lethal ingredients, or otherwise deleterious or harmful substances."*

I would rewrite the sentence: *"You are responsible to keep the jobsite clean and have a mitigation plan in place if any harmful substances are spilled."*

Unfortunately, over the years, regulations get added to over and over again. Most people don't think to delete and/or combine regulations to make them easier to read and understand.

SUMMARY: If you are in a position to make things easier by simplifying rules or regulations, DO IT!

Henry Ford

Henry Ford once said "A man who stops advertising to save money is like a man who stops a clock to save time."

Advertising comes in many forms. Some is highly effective, and some doesn't generate a single sale. Some advertising campaigns can last for years and bring in millions or even billions of dollars. Some backfire spectacularly and destroy a company.

Regardless, companies need to invest in advertising if they are going to drive new business to their doors.

Full disclosure: I'm a little biased here as my wife works in advertising so it's a bit hard to overcome confirmation bias.

I've tried to argue the alternate point: That advertising is a waste of money.

When I go down that road and start saying things like "If we cut advertising then we could invest in more machines to make more products!" I can hear the counter argument "Yes, but if we have a large inventory of products and no one knows about them, then we'll just have to rent a larger warehouse to hold them all because no one will take them off our hands."

I concede that some advertising is useless and does more harm than good…but that does not mean all advertising needs to be cut. In a time of lower sales, there's a really good chance that MORE money, not less, needs to be put into getting your message out there.

SUMMARY: Don't cut advertising budgets during a crisis. If anything, increase them.

Meetings Part 1

When you're done this chapter you might ask yourself "Where is 'Meetings Part 2'?" I didn't go farther than Part 1 because I think I could write an entire book about all the things people do wrong in meetings.

Instead, I'll start with just one quick teaser chapter:

"Don't have meetings that could have been emails."

Some "Big Announcements" do require the face-to-face of a meeting. If there are massive layoffs, that is something that a manager is going to have to do in person, not an impersonal email.

If there's really good news, like a work anniversary or a big sales win, then that might also be a good time for an in-person meeting complete with cake.

However, we have a lot of meetings that could easily be done with a simple update email. We also have a lot of emails that could have been discussed back and forth between the three people making the decision, and then the team informed. There was no reason everyone had to sit in a room and listen to three people argue with each other only to walk away from the meeting with the takeaway of: "The report is now due Tuesday and not Wednesday."

SUMMARY: Don't have meetings that could have been emails.

Retention Plan

You spend months or even years training an employee…and then they quit and go work for your competitor.

How do you stop good employees from leaving?

I've read a number of articles about this and I think a lot of them are written by people who are trying to justify and keep their own jobs. "Fun activities for team-building" will be on the list. Did someone whose job it is to organize the team-building exercises put that one on there? "Training programs" is oftentimes on the list. Did the head of corporate training slip that one on there?

Here's a list, written by people who have quit jobs, about why they quit and what the company could have done differently to keep them.

For employees to stay, the company must:

1 – Pay them well:

Don't beat around the bush here. When a hiring manager says "We have a great benefits package here" what he is really saying is "We don't pay you very much money, but you can pay for your own massage once every quarter and then get reimbursed 70% of it months later."

"Great benefits" is a way of saying "Poor pay."

Pay cmployees well. You know what a good hourly rate is. Pay them that.

2 – Show them verbal appreciation:

How much money does it cost to say during a meeting "Great job. Thanks for putting that together"?

Zero dollars. It costs you zero dollars.

So do it. Employees want verbal appreciation shown to them, especially if it's in public.

3 – Ask their opinion on things:

Are you the boss? Good. You are hopefully in that position because you are more experienced than your subordinates. Should you still ask them for their opinion? Of course you should.

For starters, it is a respectful thing to do, but more importantly it involves them in the process.

4 – Promote them / Give them bigger challenges:

This is often misinterpreted as "Dump even more things on their plate." If that's how you interpret this, then you shouldn't be a boss. People do want bigger challenges but they also don't want to be run into the ground and overworked. Give them opportunities to grow and give them opportunities to fail on their own.

5 – Mentor them:

Mentorship does not get replaced by training. Yes, formal training and continuing education is a big part of working in an evolving and dynamic world, but mentorship goes far beyond this.

Mentors guide, but they also are cheerleaders, coaches, advice givers, sounding boards, and new-goal-setters.

If you're a boss, be a mentor as well.

SUMMARY: If you want employees to stay at your company: Pay them well, show them verbal appreciation, ask their opinions on things, promote them / give them bigger challenges, and mentor them.

CEO vs. CFO

The CFO of the company is looking at the budgets and wants to know where he can cut some funding. He notices the training budget is rather high so he goes over to the CEO's office and asks: "What happens if we invest in developing our people and when they are done their training they simply leave?"

The CEO pauses and he responds: "What happens if we don't train them and they stay?"

Training is supremely important. General Electric has a massive training center in Crotonville, New York. The original campus was constructed in 1956 and the Advanced Managers' course ran for 12 weeks.

Whatever industry you are in, it is evolving every day. How are you learning and growing and how is your staff doing the same?

Many Fortune 500 companies have the luxury of their own training centers. Smaller companies pay online companies such as *Skillsoft* to produce learning management system software and content. Your company pays a monthly fee and chooses from hundreds of courses to offer that are usually centered around leadership and management. Then, your employees log in to www.skillsoft.yourcompanyname.com and can go through the learning program.

If your company isn't large enough to afford this, or if you don't work in a corporate setting, then what some small businesses do is that they send one person to a conference. When they come back they give a short presentation on what they learned. Maybe you work for a bakery – send your top baker to The Baking EXPO (yes, that's a real thing) and when they come back get them to show photos and give a short talk about what they learned.

SUMMARY: Make sure your company is continuing to invest in continuing education.

Richard Branson

Richard Branson once said "Entrepreneurship is about finding something frustrating and figuring out how to make it better."

Every single business does not need to fall into this category. Do you like baking? Do you want to open up your own bakery? That's great. Good luck.

But this is not what Branson is talking about.

Branson is talking about figuring out a solution to a problem that has never been done before and then finding a way to make money at it.

Some people start with the premise "I want to be rich." Then they move to "I'll be rich by making an app." Then they get stuck on the last part: "What should the app be?"

This way of thinking is what gets us a lot of crappy apps and useless products.

Instead, start in the opposite direction: "What is something right now that I am personally struggling with?" Then move to "Is the solution an app? Is the solution a website or is the solution a physical device that does the thing I want to do?" Create a prototype that solves your problem. If nothing else, your problem is now solved.

Finally, think to yourself: "Does anyone else suffer from this same problem? If so, could I sell them my solution?" This is the order in which you should do entrepreneurship – sadly, most people do it in the exact opposite way. This leads to failed businesses and millions of products that are pretty much useless.

SUMMARY: Start with a problem and figure out its solution. If you can sell that solution to others, you can be an entrepreneur. Do NOT start with the goal of selling something and then try to figure out what to sell.

Sorry...

I apologize for any typos or misspelled words you may have found in this book. "Doesn't MS Word check for spellcheck?" you might ask. Well, I literally had the spellcheck in my MS Word stop working while I was writing this book. I could type asdfasdfasfd and it wouldn't underline it in red as being a nonsense word.

Also, I self-published on Amazon.com and no one proofread any of this or helped me format it before it went online…so I apologize for some of the slang I've used, my sometimes odd sentence construction, plus the formatting – I tried my best.

Sorry :(

Epilogue

Thank you so much for reading this book! It means the world to me.

It takes months to plan out a book and put pen to paper. Sometimes the words flowed onto the page and other times it was a struggle to write a single sentence.

I've stood on the backs of multiple geniuses to write this book as many of the pieces of advice came from the many people I've encountered over my career.

When writing a story, it's the job of the author to be interesting. When writing non-fiction, it's the job of the writer to be informative and accurate. But when writing a book that is literally trying to tell you how to live your life via multiple bite-sized pieces of advice, I tried to make it my job to do it in a polite but direct manner. I don't want to come off as a jerk or a know-it-all. I know that I've personally struggled with many of the things that this book talks about.

If you read this book, there's a chance you bought it because you're a friend of mine and you were supporting me. Thanks! Feel free to send me an email and give me more advice that I should put in the second issue.

If you've never met me and you bought this book because you wanted some help in life, I truly hope it brought you some. I tried to price it so that it would be highly accessible, and I tried to write on a wide variety of topics so you would find at least a few of them useful.

If you and I aren't yet friends, and you want to add some advice to a future edition, please use the contact page on my website:

www.SelfTaughtMBA.com

Also, if you want more books to read, check out the list on that website – hopefully you'll find some gems.

Thanks again for reading this book. It makes me so happy to know that it's helping people because after all that was my original goal :)

Grant

Summary of Summaries

There are advice books that give everything away in the title of each chapter. There's really no point in reading the whole chapter when you can just read a single sentence that summarizes the whole thing. However, just reading one sentence will not necessarily drive the point home.

If I told a child to look both ways before they cross the road, they might do it, they might not. If I go on to explain the horrors of getting run over by a car and show them how hard it is to spot a small child and even if they are seen it's really hard to stop a car, then the message hits home. Still, the summary of "look both ways before you cross a road" is the message.

In keeping with that spirit, I specifically made the titles of each chapter of this book quite vague, but I did summarize the chapter at the end. I did not even put "Summary of Summaries" in the Table of Contents of this book because I was afraid people would flip to it and none of the pieces of advice would hit home.

Each chapter I devoted the number of pages/words to that I felt was the right number to make the point. I didn't want to be too short or too long – just right.

Congratulations for making it to the end of this book. I really hope you didn't just skip to this part.

If you did, please consider my example of "look both ways before you cross the road" – it's life-saving advice that may not be taken seriously if you don't read the whole chapter to drive the message home.

If you read each chapter in detail, I encourage you to use a pen and mark up the remaining pages. Maybe star the ones you need to work on, put a check mark besides the ones you've got locked down, and even put an X besides the ones you disagree with – you can leave a comment on www.SelfTaughtMBA.com on the "Contact" page and let me know what I'm saying is wrong and how you think I should change it for future editions of this book.

Thanks for reading…here's the summary of the summaries:

Section One: Improving Yourself

Personal Motto Part 1
Do what you're good at to make the world a better place.

Bookworm Part 1
Spend more time reading books.

Arnold
Stop drinking alcohol and coffee, stop smoking, stop taking drugs, start exercising and start eating healthy.

Heart Attack
Don't wait for a heart attack to start living healthy (literal or figurative or both).

Maintenance
Get that minor surgery or procedure that you've been putting off.

Levels
Continuously adjust the levels of where you are focusing your time, energy, and efforts.

Jesus
Make sure you have your shit figured out before you start telling people how to live their life.

Optimization
Optimize the tasks that you do repeatably in order to save time, lesson frustration, and overall improve your life.

Reflections
Every day/week/month/year, spend an appropriate amount of time reflecting on your day/week/month/year. Think about where you are and where you want to be.

No Service
You need to disconnect occasionally. Turn the phone off. I do a two to three weeks per year no-phone vacation, plus one day a week (Sunday), plus an hour or so a day with no access to a phone. You need to do this to keep your sanity.

GQ
Buy better clothes. Get a proper haircut and keep it clean. Exercise and actually care about the way you look. Stop being a slob.

Audiobooks
Start listening to audiobooks. Maybe do it during your commute, while cooking/cleaning, or while exercising.

Mistakes were Made
Learn from other's mistakes and keep a list of things NOT to do.

Diversify
Always be learning new skills and gaining new knowledge. It does not have to have anything to do with your job. Learning new things is good for your brain and makes your problem-solving skills increase.

Go Outside
Spend more time outdoors.

Bookworm Part 2
Not every book you read needs to be non-fiction. Read fictional stories that have a moral to teach, and also read fictional stories that are just a good fun read with no deeper meaning.

Expanding Your Knowledge
Broaden your knowledge beyond what you are used to immersing yourself in. Don't be proud of not knowing something or not being interested in certain things. It's ok to have favorites, but it's also always ok to learn new things about subjects you don't care for.

Ronnie Coleman
You only need to change things up when things aren't working. If you're happy with the current results, then keep doing what you're doing. This advice may seem to obvious, but people still don't listen to it.

Pain and Pleasure
People do more to avoid pain than they do to gain pleasure. Use this fact to convince yourself that you need to go through that painful thing (quitting smoking/drinking/drugs, breaking up with that loser/psycho, quitting that bad job) and you deserve that pleasure that waits at the end of the rainbow.

Buddha
Read a couple of books about Buddhism.

Lao Tzu Part 1
Remember that we need ups and downs in our lives. No one lives a life that is happiness 24/7.

Lao Tzu Part 2
Always, in every circumstance, respect one another. If people don't show you respect, you turn the other check and you show them even more respect. Know your limit as well and always be ready to walk away and quit.

I know I'm Right
Play Devil's Advocate with yourself on a regular basis.

Personal Motto Part 2
Always think of the consequences. Start planning now for the 1, 5, and 10 years from now version of you.

Happiness
Remember that success does not bring happiness – happiness brings success.

Ayn Rand

Don't be a jerk. It's ok to have your principles and your lines that you won't cross, but you don't have to be annoying or rude or a jerk about it. Let's all try to be more polite and respectful to one another.

Giving Back

Find ways to give back. Charity, volunteer work, or even just calling a relative. Let's make the world a better place.

Section Two: Career Building

Networking

Join several associations and/or committees. It will help you network so you have job security, and it will improve your standing at your own company.

VIPs

Create a list of "Big Shots" that you've met in the company and reach out to them to see if you can be on their team and help them. Eventually, they will become a mentor and help you in return.

Career Arc

Break your career up into 5-year chunks. Every 5 years it's time for a big move…hopefully upwards, but maybe laterally.

Awards & Thankyous

Thank your team members and coworkers. Bring positivity to the group even when others bring negativity. If the negativity or lack of praise continues, go work for a different company.

Cashing Out

Try to work with the jerks in your life, whether they be clients or coworkers. However, you may need to eventually say goodbye to a client or quit your job if things never get better.

Getting Kicked

Your great idea is not always going to be celebrated by others. You need to develop a thick skin and become fantastic at getting kicked during a meeting.

Strengths & Weaknesses Part 1

Play to your strengths. Find the area you are good at and a job that fits those skill sets. Strengthen your weaknesses, but realize that some things you will never be good at. Strengthen those things that are manageable and fixable.

Strengths & Weaknesses Part 2

Your strength is your weakness: Impressing people with your certificates (your strength) can make you look like a show-off and people won't want to work with you. Lead with solutions to the problem, not self-congratulations. Your strength is your weakness: If you have a weakness (a stutter, dyslexia, shyness) you can use it to your advantage. Read Malcolm Gladwell's "David and Goliath" for a full discussion of how to do this.

Stages

When working on a big project, get yes/no from your boss at multiple stages and don't wait for the final product to get a review. Make sure they are actually looking at it and opening your PDF attachment. When you want to create a big change at work, weigh the benefits of keeping everything a secret vs. involving everyone. Think about the personalities that you work for and answer the question: Would they be pissed off if I did this in secret? Or would they be impressed?

Massive Frustration

Remember that massive success usually does not come without massive frustration.

Forbes

Set HUGE goals. Come up with a plan for how to get there. You will most likely fail to hit your original goal – climbing Mount Everest, becoming a billionaire, or being President – but you will most likely succeed in getting in better shape, making more money, or getting elected to local office.

Fruit

When you're green you grow, when you ripen you rot. Make sure to keep pushing yourself to learn new things and develop your skills. Don't stay in your rut forever.

Easing in and Out

Whether it's a change in a company-wide system, a job promotion, retirement, or simply a way that you do your day-to-day work, make sure to ease into it. This gives your coworkers time to adjust and if done properly, people won't even notice it or complain at all.

Bridge Burning
No matter how hard it may be to keep your cool, never ever ever burn a bridge. End on a high note in every situation. It doesn't matter if it will never come back to haunt you; that's not the point. Be a good person, not a bad person. Never burn a bridge.

Writing
Attempt to write a book or an article or a paper. It'll be a fantastic experience even if it never gets off the ground and you are the only person that reads it. Just give it a try.

Pivot!
Pivot your skillsets. You are good at X, so use it to help you out doing Y.

Celebrated
Don't stay where you're tolerated, go where you're celebrated!

Value vs. Necessity
Learn the difference between jobs that fulfill necessity and jobs that add value. Try to craft your position into one that does both.

Burning the Midnight Oil
Stop working 18-hour days. No one is impressed and your only reward will be that your boss will give you more work. Work a solid 9-5, Monday-to-Friday, then take a break. You'll probably actually end up being MORE productive.

Section Three:
Communicating with Others

Angry Angry Hippos

Never send an email or text message while you are angry. Cool down and sleep on it. Maybe don't even send it at all or at least proof read it and reword it before you send it.

To CC Bcc

Fill in the "To", "CC", and "Bcc" fields as the last thing you do before you send an email to avoid accidentally hitting send with an email that isn't finished yet.

Sayonara

Make sure you have full automatic email signatures set up on your phone and your laptop.

Subpoena

Always assume that everything you write and/or say will one day maybe end up in court or on the front cover of the Wall Street Journal. Are you proud of what you said? Could you at least defend it?

LOUD NOISES

Remember that data wins arguments, not raised voices.

J

Don't just talk to certain people when you need to get something out of them. You're not being a friend – you're being a parasite.

Saving Face

Give someone an out. Allow them to save face. Don't make people feel stupid in front of their peers.

The Idiot in the Room
When someone is incompetent and feels insecure because they are unable to contribute, ask them simple questions or give them simple tasks so they can feel like a big man.

Feeling Smart
Make others feel smart and look good to their boss.

Proper Email Technique
The basic format of every email that intends on asking a question goes like this:
1) This is my question
2) Here is some background information that may help you in answering it
3) I'm ending the email by re-asking the question to you

The basic format of every email that intends on telling someone bad news goes like this:
1) Here's our understanding of what you wanted to have happen
2) Here's all the things that we got accomplished
3) Here's what happened to stop us from achieving our goal
4) Here's what we are going to do to make things right

Email Etiquette Part 4
Learn the difference between Reply and Reply-All buttons in email.

Ghost Phone Calls
Politely introduce yourself, make small talk, and use Ghost Phone Calls when people don't take you seriously. Worst case scenario, use actual phone calls to the boss.

Keep it Simple
Don't use ten words when nine words will work.

Disagreeing
Disagree with people, but do it in a professional, polite, and respectful manner. Stop beating around the bush. If you disagree with someone, keep it short and don't sugar coat it. People will appreciate your honesty.

Come Together

When negotiating, try to see things from other people's perspectives and work towards a common goal.

Quiet Time

Only send emails and make phone calls between the hours of 9:00 am and 5:00 pm, Monday to Friday. If you want to be an even better person, only email/call between 10:00 am and 4:00 pm and never call during lunch hour.

Use Your Words

Call people on the phone. Emails can come off as stiff, demanding, and rude. Call people first, then follow up with an email that summarizes what you called about.

Communication Breakdown

When someone compliments you, take it as a compliment. Don't dissect exactly how they said it and try to find ways to get mad about it. Let it go. They thanked you, they complimented you. Take the win and move on.

Shitting

Know your shit, and know when you are shit.

Let it Go

Evaluate your stories, phrases, and everything that comes out of your mouth. Do you repeat them often? It's time to get some new stories. It's time to let the old ones go.

Singing in the Shower

Use your alone time to practice phrases, sentences, and even entire stories/arguments in your head multiple times before you debut them in public.

Winning and Losing

You don't have to win every argument. Don't be that guy. Sometimes (or a lot of the times) let other people win.

Reaching Out

Connect with people who you've maybe fallen out of touch with. Bury the hatchet if there was some bad blood there. Let's come together as a world.

Sunshine & Rainbows

Be the person that shares good news with everyone. Let someone else be the person that tells the office about the bad news.

Section Four: How to be Ultra Productive

Pain then Pleasure
On your to-do list, alternate from doing the things you hate the most, with the things you really actually want to do. Pain, then pleasure. Repeat.

You've Got Mail
Respond to messages instantly. Either unsubscribe, answer the question, point them to someone else, or give them an estimate on when you'll be able to answer the email in detail.

Keep Chipping Away
Try to choose projects that don't go in reverse when they are neglected for a period of time. Keep chipping away at them, and eventually you'll finish.

Biting & Chewing
At points in your life you need to make sure you aren't biting off more than you can chew. Slow things down, take a breath, and take time for yourself. However, if you've been coasting for a long time, it may be that you need to start biting off more than you can chew. Flip between these two states throughout your life – don't stay in one forever.

Homebody Part 1
Ask your boss if you can work from home.

Homebody Part 2
When working from home, internally make sure you are in a good professional routine and treat this seriously. Externally, make sure you are keeping in regular touch with the team.

Why do we Win?
Success comes from the combination of three things: Luck, Hard work, and Willingness to Act. Luck comes and goes, hard work we seem to be willing to put the time into, but we must also be willing to act when an opportunity comes along.

Albert Einstein

Clean up and simplify your life.

Record Keeping

Back things up. Save constantly. Record important things. Make lists of stats and track records. Update your resume and keep on top of things.

Billionaires

No one tells billionaires that their idea is stupid. Rarely does someone tell their boss how dumb his idea is. If you want real feedback on your idea, ask people who make more money than you, are higher up the corporate food chain, or are completely disconnected from you. Then you can get some actual feedback.

Running

It's easy to go for a run when it's sunny out – but it's not always sunny. You need to find motivation to cross things off your to-do list without waiting for the "perfect time" to do them…because the "perfect time" may never come.

Section Five: How to Manage a Project

Coach vs. Captain

Teams need Captains – active contributors that are experts in their field; and they also need Coaches – cheerleaders, motivators, and people who can take a step back and see the big picture. Figure out what your team needs and when your team needs it, and don't give them the opposite of what they need, which is a Coach who is on the court and a Captain who is on the bench.

Chains

Tell people the end goal, then let them figure out their own path. Take the chains off. They may surprise you with a new innovation.

...but it comes heated up

Remember that not everything has to fit into the perfect set of preset rules. However, also remember that there may be a good reason for that seemingly dumb rule and make sure to seek it out before you break it.

Iterations

Involve your client early on when you are coming up with your proposal. Don't wait until your proposal is perfected to finally present it – you may be way out to lunch and nowhere even close to what they were thinking.

Real Progress

Don't confuse "Motion" with "Progress."

Young Drivers

"Make everything your onion." Just because you might not technically be in charge of it, remember that you're on the same ship as the rest of the team.

Task Master

Don't delegate – Leverage instead.

Move On

At each decision point, ask yourself of the various options "Is it safe? Is it legal? Is it ethical? If it's a "yes" to all three, then you have every right to choose that option and move on. Keep the ship going forward.

Cleaning Crew

When cleaning something up (whether literal or figuratively) start with the cleanest item that still needs just a bit more cleaning. Continue to clean from cleanest to dirtiest. Do not start by tackling the big issue or the dirtiest item. Cleanest to dirtiest, top to bottom.

Steve Jobs

Make sure the hidden parts of your product or service are just as beautiful and polished as the parts you intend for your client to see.

Schedule Budget Quality

Start with a schedule, calculate a budget, and build in quality checks.

Section Six:
How to Improve Your Work Life

Whack-a-Mole
As much as you can, treat each new task like the game "Whack-a-Mole." Whack those tasks so they don't start multiplying.

The Riddler
If you're smart, make sure that you rise up, cash out, or adapt.

Figure it Out
Don't ask your boss questions – instead, present problems with what you think the solution is and ask for input.

Three Strengths
Experience, Knowledge, and Boldness – Best case scenario you have all three, but if you lack in one area you must make up for it in the others.

Gorilla George
Consolidate your mistakes and questions to a small group of people.

Infectious
Remember that both positivity and negativity are infectious. You can spread both to others, so try to focus on the positive and the world will be a better place.

Leave the Room
The moment you are the smartest person in the room, you are the dumbest. Join a team or a group of friends that push you to new heights, not ones that drag you down.

Cooking Eggs

Take a chance and break a few eggs – you have to if you ever want to make an omelet. And also remember that it's easier to ask for forgiveness than it is to ask for permission.

Remembering

Don't make people ask you twice. Create a list of to-dos, and don't have multiple lists all over the place. Have one list that you chip away at.

Fires

Remember that the world does not revolve around you, and your fire is not necessarily as hot as someone else's fire – we've all got fires to put out.

The Nose Job

Don't let it be so easy for other people to rattle you. Don't get your nose out of joint at every little thing. You have the power to be annoyed or let things go.

Backup Plan

You always need a backup plan, or multiple backup plans. It doesn't matter what the situation is – have backup plans.

Weekend Plans

Always have a somewhat reasonably interesting answer to the question: "What are you planning this weekend?"

First Boss

Always have an answer to the three questions of: What have you got done so far?; What are you currently working on?; and What do you want to get done?

Emotional Intelligence

Read more books to help develop your Emotional Intelligence.

Section Seven: Leadership

Politics, Law, Psychology, and Babysitting
Gain knowledge in politics, law, psychology, and babysitting.

Rick and Morty
Don't be a jerk. Just because you are smart or the boss does not mean you have to be mean about it.

Jack Welch
Every manager must have good energy, energize their team, have a competitive edge, and execute the deliverable.

Getting Results
Vision with a Plan, plus Drive, plus Patience, equals Results.

Who's Responsible?
Remember that when you are "Responsible" for something that not only gives you the right to make decisions, but it also gives you the duties that come along with it. Responsibility equals rights+duties.

Leadership
If you are trying to become a leader, ask yourself if you are able to get other people to grow and/or succeed. If you aren't, then those are skills you need to work on and can be found by reading more books on leadership.

Mushroom Management
Don't do the following things to you staff: Keep them in the dark about the big picture, shit on their ideas, or straight-up ignore them.

Section Eight: Running a Company

ENRON: Behavior vs. Performance

Do not tolerate bad behavior, even if it's from a high-performer…unless you want to become ENRON, a cheater, a wife-beater, or a drug addicted criminal.

Internal, External, Technological

We are prepared for technological challenges, we can figure out external challenges and even enjoy them if we treat them like a game, but the real challenge is to kill off unnecessary levels of internal approvals that slow innovation.

Creating Change

The five elements of Change in a corporation are Vision, Skills, Incentives, Resources, and an Action Plan.

Safety First

If you're in charge of safety on a job site, make it practical and don't make people wear PPE when it actually makes them less safe. If you're in charge of safety in an office, make is applicable to an office, not a doomsday scenario. Make all forms one-page max. Finally, safety gear should be brand new, high-quality, fashionable, comfortable, readily available, and totally free.

Talk is Cheap

Put the same emphasis on production as you do on sales. Celebrate good reviews, because good quality work is more important than a sales pitch and will create repeat customers.

Fishing

Be proud of the price, quantity, and quality of what you are selling to someone. Don't pull the wool over anyone's eyes. If they don't actually need the product, don't try to upsell it to them. Don't sell water to a fish.

Four Groups of Employees

If you're a boss who gives annual reviews, put your employees into one of four categories: "Keeping doing what you're doing", "Do more of what you're doing", "Do something different", or "Leave the company."

Leap Frog

If you are in the upper management position to do so, foster an environment where employees are encouraged to communicate horizontally across the corporation with people in multiple different offices without having to go through a series of bosses. Also encourage an environment where a junior employee can bring up an idea to a senior employee who is multiple corporate levels above them.

Cannibals

Don't be afraid to cannibalize your products. If you don't, you competitor will.

The Art of War

Foster an environment of happiness at work.

Machiavelli

Make sure every job is needed. If your job is to think up creative ways as to why you need to keep your job, then I'm sorry, but you should not have a job.

Hoop Jumping

If you are in a position to make things easier by simplifying rules or regulations, DO IT!

Henry Ford

Don't cut advertising budgets during a crisis. If anything, increase them.

Meetings Part 1

Don't have meetings that could have been emails.

Retention Plan

If you want employees to stay at your company: Pay them well, show them verbal appreciation, ask their opinions on things, promote them / give them bigger challenges, and mentor them.

CEO vs. CFO

Make sure your company is continuing to invest in continuing education.

Richard Branson

Start with a problem and figure out its solution. If you can sell that solution to others, you can be an entrepreneur. Do NOT start with the goal of selling something and then try to figure out what to sell.

THE END

Grant Waldie, B.A.Sc.
www.SelfTaughtMBA.com

This space is for your notes

This space is for your notes

This space is for your notes

This space is for your notes

Made in the USA
Middletown, DE
15 May 2020